Ruminating on Sloth

AND OTHER INDULGENCES

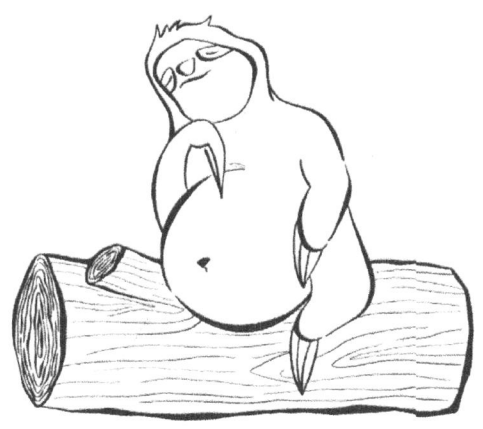

©2020 John Shields

All Rights Reserved.

TABLE OF CONTENTS

INTRODUCTION	1
NAMEWORTHY	5
Who's Lionized Barry More?	6
Where Never Is Heard a Disparaging Word	8
Don't Forget Rufus T. Firefly	11
Clues Blues	14
Blackie the Crow	16
TASKS	19
The Seventh Seal (Attempt)	20
The Least Essential Chore Contest	23
Lawn and Laundryf	25
BEFORE THE CLOUD	27
And We Wonder Where the Time Goes?	28
K, Too (Not the Mountain)	31
CHEESES	33
That Is a Crock, Madame	34
Deviled Parmesan	36
LANGUAGE	39
Iamb Inspired	40
SM Editors	43
Freedom of Mis-Expression	46
Cross Words for the Crossword	49
Of Greek Philosophers and Jalapenos	52
POETRY I	55
Poetry the Easy Way	56
SPECIAL DELIVERER	59
Being Santa's Helper Has Its UPS and Downs	60
FedEx's Secret Weapon	64
FINDINGS I	67
Exploding Ink and Tipsy Monkeys	68
FAMILY	71
Mac, Our Finch	72

Chloe Graduates	75
Teeth Wisdom	78
By Definition … My Dad	81
A Friend for All Seasons Is Gone	84
Tending the Headstone	86

LOCALS — 89

Maya Mole	90
The Delaware Deluge Sympathy Card	92
The Philadelphia Parking Authority and Its Co-conspirator, the Bureau of Administrative Adjudication.	94
Is It Possible I've Found My Soul Mate?	97

DOCTORING — 101

Shot Flu and Flu	102
My Standard Deviation	104
Take My Epidermis … Please!	107

POETRY II — 109

Poetry: The Sequel	110

PERSPECTIVE — 113

Ruminating on Sloth	114
Reunion, Reconsideration	117
Notes From a Backyard Stargazer	120
When Black Holes Have Earth for Lunch	122
The Serious World of The New Testament	125

DEUCE — 127

"Not the Pictures, John!"	128
Ab Crunches for Tabby?	131

FINDINGS II — 135

How Komodo Dragons Affect the Fishing Industry	136

DIY — 139

If Fencing Referred Only to Swords	140
Call Me WC Shields	143
Water on the Brain	145

SPORTS: BASEBALL — 149

The Duel	150
Lacrosse vs. Baseball: No Contest	153

Questionable Reporting on the Fly	155
When Hitting Instruction Isn't Part of the Job Description	158
SPORTS: NON-BASEBALL	**161**
Hash Marks, Yes; Stretch Marks, Never	162
The Next Great American Spectacle?	164
Volunteering for the Chain Gang	167
SELF	**169**
Balms Away	170
IQ Fraud	173
Mi Stressa Es Su Stressa	176
When Terrycloth Gets Threadbare, I've Done My Job	179
POETRY III	**183**
Poetry: Could It Be Verse?	184
CULTURE	**187**
Doghouse Deductions	188
Summer Camps for Structured Lives	191
INTERNATIONAL	**193**
Wal-Martihuacan and Other Signs of the Apocalypse	194
My Lawless Province Getaway	196
FALALA	**199**
As Crèches Go	200
"Tinsel"? or "Icicles"?	202
PITS	**205**
Rupert's Gift	206
A New York Doll	210
My "Jazz"-ercise Workout	212
FINDINGS III	**215**
Unicorns in North Korea? Why Not?	216
EVERYDAY THINGS	**219**
They Can't Place the Face	220
ACKNOWLEDGEMENTS	**223**
ABOUT THE AUTHOR	**224**

To my dictionary-loving father, John Shields.

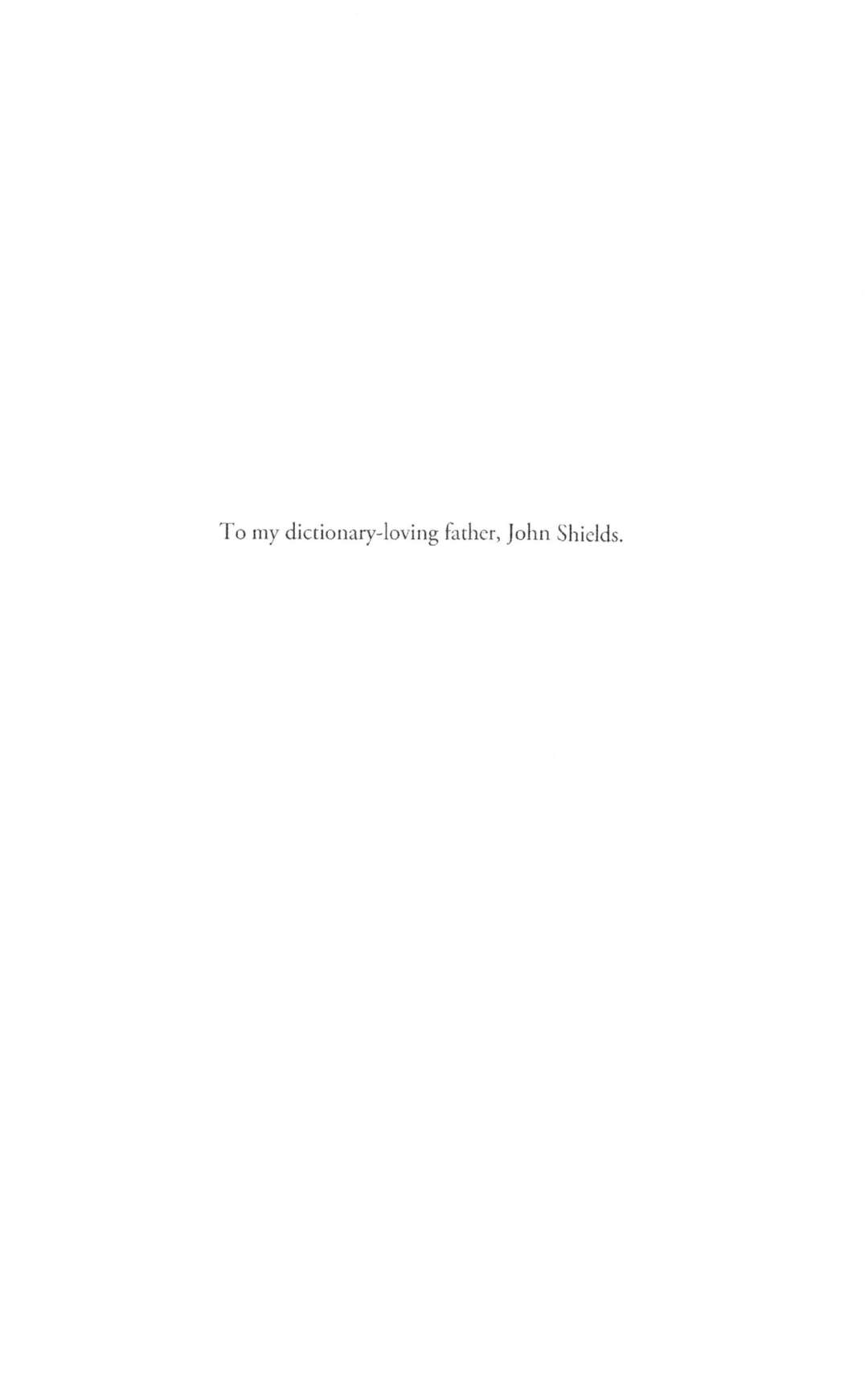

INTRODUCTION

The columns in this collection were written between 2004 and 2010. Each has been amended slightly to include an introductory remark by the writer – much like this one, only funnier.

Dear reader,

At the height of my literary powers, this is how I described myself:

Intelligent, witty, literate, original ... just some of the words that maybe someday they'll use to describe me, as opposed to what I currently get: affable, spells correctly, doesn't bother anybody.

I came to column writing serendipitously. The opportunity arose shortly – very shortly – minutes shortly – after I was hired to coach varsity baseball at New Hope-Solebury High School in Pennsylvania's fabled Bucks County, a scenic locale nestled along the Delaware River whose literary tradition – Michener, Parker, Kaufmann et al. – was about to be cheapened by my arrival.

Three of us were vying for the coaching job, none of us named Michener, Parker, or Kaufmann. There was me of course, a fellow who had never coached baseball before, and the golf coach. Wait, you're thinking, that makes two of you, so how did you get the job?

Fortunately, the athletic director was up on his misplaced modifiers and offered me the position.

I was 55 and had never coached a high school team. But yes, I had coached baseball before.

I barely had time to shape the brim of my new NHS Lions cap when Scott Edwards, the editor of the local newspaper, the *New Hope Gazette*, called to set up a next-day interview to learn more about the high school's new, geriatric baseball coach. I mentioned that I was a writer. Scott suggested there might be a column for me, naively envisioning a coach's-eye view on community sports.

As was true of my high school coaching experience, I had never been a columnist either. But I was published, with a couple of op-eds in the *Philadelphia Inquirer*. Neither came within a Yankee pinstripe of the community sports angle, but Scott liked them and offered a "Let's see what happens" agreement.

I recognize desperation when I see it.

So, within the space of 24 hours I became a varsity baseball head coach and a weekly commentary page columnist.

Every columnist and baseball coach has a style, an approach. In researching collections of columns, I noticed it was common for the columnist to apologize for the unavoidably dated nature of the topics and people that were the original subjects. I tried to avoid that position by committing to keeping my subject matter as universal in time and content as possible.

Because of that, as you read, you'll be reacquainted with some names and topics, most of which still have a recognition factor 10-15 years later.

So get ready to say hello again to Martin Luther, Yao Ming, Dave Barry, Mary, Mother of God, "Survivor," Norton Antivirus, Osama bin Laden *and* Ayman al-Zawahiri, digital cameras, Pedro Martinez, Stephen Hawking, Laura Bush, Aristotle, the lawless provinces, VCRs, Intelligent Design, Nancy Grace, and Mordecai "Three Fingers" Brown. (I know ... who?)

May they all find new homes in the digital files of you, this new group of readers. And if you're a returning reader from the *Gazette* days ... Mordecai will be pleased to see you.

Wrapping up the story of my twofold employment path in New Hope ...

The coaching job lasted two years or nine helicopter parents – whichever came first. You can guess which came first. My column, though, ran in the paper weekly until the *Gazette* died five years later, and online intermittently for about another year. Scott Edwards christened it "Everyday Things," and it provided commentary and smiles to a community and region long recognized for its artistic character. I am honored to be part of the newspaper's history.

As for writing the column from which this book's contents derive, it's these words of the great 18th-century writer and lexicographer Dr. Samuel Johnson, that, along with "ruminating," always seemed to pop into my head:

"The two most engaging powers of an author are to make new things familiar and familiar things new."

I tried to do that on every page of my pieces for the *Gazette*, while having as much fun with our language as my brain would allow.

NAMEWORTHY

I thought this was one of the cleverest titles I ever came up with. My editor thought "Who's Lionized Barry?" was better.

Who's Lionized Barry More?

If you want to see silly human behavior in action, put a bunch of newspaper columnists in a room with a bar and invite Dave Barry to mingle with them.

For those of you unfamiliar with Dave Barry – and, hard to believe, there are a few of you out there – he is the Pulitzer Prize-winning columnist from the *Miami Herald* who is to humor columnists as Moby Dick is to the general whale population.

Dave was a featured speaker at this year's annual conference of the National Society of Newspaper Columnists. The conference was held in my hometown, Philadelphia.

It opened with a reception at the Pen & Pencil Club, the oldest, continuously operating press club in America except for Gold's Gym. I was an early arriver, so I had Benjamin Franklin to myself for awhile. (Around here, Ben always makes an appearance at conventions like these.)

It's neat meeting someone famous. I gave Ben my autograph and let him pose for a picture with me before steering him in the direction of other famous people.

The room had filled by now and things were going pretty much as you'd expect: drinking and mingling, minking and dringling. All of a sudden, I noticed Dave Barry had arrived.

I wasn't sure it was him at first. It was pretty early in the evening for a celebrity to arrive, though I'd gotten there around 4. Dave must've heard about the complimentary buffet too.

(Here's a little secret about Dave Barry: He's a Heineken drinker. At least we can infer as much from the five I bought him throughout the evening.

He didn't buy me a drink, but I think that was only because he couldn't get close enough to the bar to order me one.)

As word spread that Dave Barry was in the room, people began exhibiting the oddest behavior. Patting themselves to make sure they'd brought their digital cameras with them, they began disengaging from whomever they were talking with at the moment to glance urgently in Dave's direction, who, by this time, was pretending to ignore the columnist from the *Springfield Keen Observer* clinging to his right thigh.

One by one, they began making their way across the room to him, often abandoning their conversational partner in mid-sen...

Soon, a line had formed behind the prostrated *Observer* columnist. The first in line was prodding the columnist on the floor to hurry up and finish his adulation.

"Whadya think we have? All night?"

Meanwhile a female columnist from the *Sarasota Post Menopause* had feigned tripping over the Thigh Clinger so that she could fall into Dave's arms. This ploy didn't succeed because Dave was busy at the time receiving the first two Heinekens I'd bought him and didn't have a free hand. She fell into the arms of Ben Franklin instead, who'd mistakenly taken Dave for the famous general interest columnist from the *Erie Morning Sun*.

I'd brought my own digital camera in case something snapworthy came up. This seemed a good time, so I whispered to Dave that I'd be more than happy to pose for a picture with him later, after things had quieted down. His frozen smile told me he was grateful for the offer.

A columnist from the *Dubuque Tribune Daily Advocate Times* volunteered to take a picture of Dave and me with my camera, which she did, and it came out nicely. Dave is seen leaning toward me in an effort to close the four-foot gap between us, but I think, overall, it works.

"It was big of her to offer to take our picture," I opined to a fellow from the *St. Paul Epistle*. I said that I thought she'd been at times picayune.

"No," he corrected me. "She's been with the *Tribune* her whole career."

Never, never, never. Fret, fret, fret.

Where Never Is Heard a Disparaging Word

I don't know Maira Kalman personally, but her biography states that she's an established illustrator, designer, and author who's done several covers for *The New Yorker*, whereas I can't even get a headshot in the *New Hope Gazette* so who am I to even bring this up?

For the past year, Ms. Kalman has been doing a monthly "column" online for the *New York Times*, each consisting of about 20 illustrations and her accompanying thematic reflections. Her current effort, we're told, is her last before taking a little break.

At the bottom of this scrolling work of art, readers (viewers?) are invited to leave comments.

Regrettably, many accepted.

> *Come Sunday I, your faithful reader, will dress up quite formally, go sit in a proper Parisian café and nibble on bouchées à la Reine. And, as in the name of these delights, I will salute my Queen (that's you) of artistic pursuit.* (Comment by Lia)

> *Time stands still when reading your column and one has a chance to breath in and out slooowly, travel inward and become teary eyed with the sweetness of an opened heart/mind. Thank you for being.* (Comment by Pema)

> *Never leave your hotel or return without chocolate cake!*
> *Never fail to smile at people who are missing teeth!*
> *Never forget those little space/times rubbings of separate ecosystems!*
> (Comment by Bob)

And goochie goochie gumdrop to you, Bob.

I happened to catch Kalman's latest effort when it was hot off the cyber presses and had as yet received only a dozen or so comments. Finding her work – let alone her admirers' comments – too cloying for my own tastes, I left my own comment.

Granted, it had some sting, like when I asked if I was supposed to know who Pina Bausch is and is she related to Pina Grigio. But I really did strive to be articulate and worthy of the *Times*.

A message appeared telling me, "Your comment is awaiting moderation."

Moderation, as in softening any rough edges, filtering obscenities or personal attacks, things like that. Nothing I was guilty of – except possibly when I suggested that Pema and Bob, commenters 2 and 3 respectively, were audience plants.

By next morning, the number of posted comments had increased from 14 to 183.

Mine wasn't among them.

I skimmed the lot of them and found *there wasn't a negative comment in the bunch!* "What are the odds of that?" I thought.

That thought became the opening sentence of my second comment.

This time around, I wrote that c'mon, no artist is universally admired and that a little "constructive contrarianism" ought to be welcomed, not censored. What artist worth her salt wouldn't agree? I told Maira that I didn't like her propensity for dropping obscure cultural references like Pina Bausch and "coulibiacs" and for making statements like "There is no better start to a party than a puff pastry."

I praised her illustrations, but that didn't help. My second comment failed to make the cut, too.

"Leave (only positive) comments," the invitation should have read. This wasn't a forum for artistic feedback. This was a forum for jaw-dropping idol worship and bad writing.

> OH DEAR! Fret, fret, fret ... Ah, at least I love summer as much as I love your monthly posting, so perhaps it won't be so bad for me that you are taking a break. I LOVE that you are having a book! To

have a book is a wonderful thing. You are a wonderful thing! Ah, there are so many wonderful things ... summer and books and you! (Comment by Lee)

Hark the flush of the pissoir, Lee.

Undaunted, I tried a different approach. Since I'd used my true name twice, I figured the moderation machine might recognize it a third time, so I left a comment under the pseudonym "Sara Point" and used my son's teen-flavored email address:

Wow, your stuff is really good, Maira.

I'm in, at 190.

I shall celebrate with a puff pastry.

Groucho's movie character names couldn't have done better.

Don't Forget Rufus T. Firefly

Workers in countless offices across America make lists of the funny names they encounter. This is especially true for those whose jobs expose them to lots of names. I had a job like that in college, when I worked for Sears in their credit center. The phones rang steadily, with salespersons calling for credit approval and customers calling with various inquiries or complaints. My co-workers and I handled the calls, and behind every one of them was a name – from time to time a very funny name.

Relative to the general population, there aren't many funny names, and within the population of funny names, there aren't many that have Sears accounts, let alone a reason to call about them, so our particular list took a long time to grow. Plus, we were college students with discriminating taste when it came to funny things. We didn't accept just any name that came along with a snicker attached to it.

The names you're about to read, then, are the elite, the *crème de la crème*. They belong to otherwise ordinary people who were only looking to buy a new refrigerator, perhaps, or question a finance charge. People just like you and me – except for one unfortunate difference.

I list them for you by category because I find categorizing a helpful tool for recalling things. Normal names usually defy categorization. They simply *are*. But these ... these are not normal names. (And if yours is on the list, blame your parents, not me.)

> OCCUPATIONS: Deheartburn Cook and Morton Mechanic
>
> HISTORICAL: Queen Victoria West, Columbus Christopher, and Lawrence Arabia
>
> DELUSIONAL: Hannibal Cabbagetalk
>
> EXISTENTIAL: Casper Lonesome

OPPOSITES: Gary Loser and Sol Superfine

CONTRADICTION IN TERMS: Net Gross and Geronimo Pacifico

RHYMERS: Clyde Hyde, Frank Blank, and Dumi Lumi

BREASTS: Daniel Titz and Robert Teats

THANKS, MOM AND DAD: Lucille LaSalle, Opin Houser, and Meyer Weiner

SEXUAL ORIENTATION: Peter Homo and Fairy Raymond

WAS THE MIDDLE INITIAL REALLY NECESSARY: Barney B. Bus, Swift T. Benjamin, and Cecil C. Satterfield, Sr.

WEATHER: Mister Blizzard

CANNED GOODS: Ken A. Corn

BLUE CHEESE AT NIGHT, SAILOR'S DELIGHT: Hardy Curd and Norbert Saltpeter

WHEN NOT TO HYPHENATE LAST NAMES: Agnes Dingle and Boston Berry

YOU MEAN THERE'S A SENIOR TOO? Rex Tomb, Jr.

OUR FOREST FRIENDS: Hasker Hare, Bodley Buck, and Theodore Moose

VEHICLES: America Studebaker, Rodman Buggy, and Walter Pickup

FOOTWEAR: Seymour Tow

TICKLE SOUNDS: Linchy Coochi

BODILY EXCRETIONS: Isadore Pissis and Larue Lunger

NOT QUITE THE F-WORD BUT CLOSE: Ivan Fluck and R.L. Flucker

PERSONALITY TYPES: Rufus Angry, Leroy Vile, Robert Sweetie, Harry Shifty, and Superior Spence

CLASSIEST ATTEMPT TO FIX BAD LAST NAME: Wellington Wack

MOST SUCCESSFUL ATTEMPT TO FIX BAD LAST NAME: Rocky Marble

LEAST SUCCESSFUL ATTEMPT TO FIX BAD LAST NAME: Max Blob

HAPPY NAMES: Merriweather Christmas, Mary Kiss, and Sidney Seasongood

ROLE YOU COULD SEE GROUCHO PLAYING: Loren B. Hoogerhyde,

Winfield Strawhacker, Melvin Mumpower, and Spurgeon Wormley

REAL OR IMAGINARY: Playford Friend

IN A CATEGORY ALL THEIR OWN: Primes Human, Precious Purry, Saturnina Trevina, Wayne Wisdom, and Legrand Ball

And last, but not least …

MOTIVATIONAL: Attaway Brooks

When scholars cite various attributes that distinguish us from the animal kingdom, they often neglect to mention a very important one: Only humans have the ability to name.

"The particulars of the technical analysis are not something we're going to reveal."

— *Homeland Security Adviser Frances Townsend, on the intelligence community's scrutinizing of the most recent Osama bin Laden videotape.*

Clues Blues

I've been studying the recent Osama bin Laden video myself for clues to his whereabouts. Here's what *my* technical analysis has turned up:

First, those who suspect he's in the lawless provinces of Pakistan are mistaken. Notice the v-pattern that is formed by his tan robe against his white shirt. That tells me we should be looking for him in Vermont or Virginia. And we certainly shouldn't forget the Virgin Islands. He isn't.

The brown background in the video is also especially revealing. One's natural first reaction is to think, "UPS," but that's just a clever misdirection on bin Laden's part. Besides, he'd have to wear shorts in the summertime and you gotta have the legs for that.

No, Brown University. That's where we ought to be looking. Think about it:

Where is Brown located? In Providence, Rhode Island. And what is "Providence" another word for? "God." Or, just maybe ... Allah.

So, one possibility is that bin Laden is hiding in the dorm room of a student named Virginia, or maybe Ella, on the campus of Brown University.

His newly-dyed black beard bears examination as well. It could be an allusion to the famous pirate, Blackbeard, another guy who was hard to catch. If so, we might redirect our search to the West Indies, specifically Nassau in the Bahamas, where Blackbeard had his headquarters. (The lawless-province parallel is striking.)

You can't rule out Ireland, either. Why? Because when you look at Osama's black beard and the tan robe he's wearing, they're suggestive of the Black and Tans, who tormented the Irish in the early 1920s, much the way al-Qaeda torments us today.

Note to self: check and see if there's a room number "1920" in the freshman dorm at Brown.

I don't know what to make of the white headpiece bin Laden's wearing. I want to say "Seabees," but he's landlocked. Between the black beard and the white turban, though, I'm thinking maybe a piano factory. Have we searched Steinway yet? Osama's a tall guy, so spinets and baby grands are out. That would leave concert grands.

What else is in black and white? Well, everything's there in black and white, but then he wouldn't be hiding, would he?

Stevie Wonder and Paul McCartney? No, that's ebony and ivory. We already have pianos covered.

Wait. Old movies. *Casablanca*? Possibly. We should check there. Yes, especially there because "casa blanca" means "white house" and Osama is nothing if not an ironic humorist.

My technical analysis concludes with an investigation into why the spelling of his first name has changed. All of a sudden, it's "Usama." Some headline writers and commentators have even taken to referring to him as "UBL."

It's probably Obama who pushed for "Usama."

Why not call him "Binny?" B-b-b-Binny and the jet-black beard.

But wait. An aha! moment. I'm looking at that "Usama bin Laden' name more closely. If we view it as a code, might it not be saying "U.S.A. May be in L.A. 'den?" That's it! I think I found him. Round up all the movie extras, especially the ones with fake-looking black beards.

… Then there's the intelligence community's technical analysis …

There are missing-pet posters, and then there are MISSING-PET POSTERS.

Blackie the Crow

It's not often you see a missing-animal notice like the one I saw posted on a library bulletin board this week. It said:

LOST CROW

ANSWERS TO THE NAME "BLACKIE"

The flyer included a photo of the bird in profile and a phone number to call in case any of us spot him.

I imagine you're thinking what I'm thinking: What if it goes to voice mail?

Assume for a moment that Blackie really is what the photo suggests he is – someone's pet crow. First of all, crows are birds, and birds do something that missing cats and dogs don't: They fly. Blackie could be in Manitoba by now.

Next, how do I know that the bird perched above my front door as we speak isn't a raven? I've asked him if he's Blackie, but he's mute on the subject.

To help us track down Blackie and avoid confusing him with a raven, here's what my research turned up:

Blackie's lost-crow poster didn't specify his size and weight, only that he can hear, but a raven is about seven inches taller and three times heavier than a crow. So don't be thinking "porker" when you're crow-spotting.

Another distinguishing feature is that a raven's tail is wedge-shaped while a crow's is fan-shaped. By the time you can see that distinction, however, the bird would be so far above the ground that he couldn't hear you calling, "Here, Blackie."

Other physical differences to be aware of: A raven's beak is more rounded than a crow's, and its call is more guttural and hoarse, as compared to the cleaner, higher-pitched sound of a crow. Like the difference between Tom Waits and Art Garfunkel.

Ravens are also more solitary than crows, which will often assemble in large flocks. So, should a flock of crows appear on your lawn, you would have to say, "Alright, which one of you is Blackie?" That would leave you susceptible to them playing tricks on you.

"I'm Blackie."

"No, I'm Blackie."

"They're both lying. It's me that's Blackie."

You don't get these shenanigans with ravens.

As for their diet, both ravens and crows are omnivores, but ravens prefer carrion, while crows prefer check-in.

Heh-heh.

Finally, a crow's feathers are a plain, flinty black. A raven's feathers, on the other hand, shine with a blue or purple tint when the sun hits them. So your odds of finding Blackie are slimmer on a cloudy day. And forget finding him in a crow bar. The lighting in those places is meant to conceal, not reveal.

No crow profile is complete without knowing the bird's basic outlook toward scarecrows. Is he intimidated by them or does he treat them with disdain? Is he attracted to them? Does he sit on them? Does he relish pecking their eyes out? Knowing the answers to those questions might tell us if we're wasting our time searching farms.

Speaking of profiles, the one of Blackie was probably intended to show off his better side, but I'd have preferred seeing a straight-on shot as well, like the mug shots on bulletin boards at police stations. What if he walks right up to me one day while I'm down on my knees weeding? Am I going to say, "Would you mind turning your head a bit and looking over toward the shed" to a bird whose language skills are limited to answering to the name Blackie?

And if by some miracle I see the crow that actually is Blackie? Just because he answers to Blackie doesn't mean he's going to answer to me.

For Blackie's family's sake, I hope he turns up soon. It's a scary world out there. People eat crow every day.

TASKS

Ingmar Bergman's knight meets his match in the kitchen in ...

The Seventh Seal (Attempt)

In the beginning there was Saran Wrap. Then came HandiWrap, made, not begotten, of its own substance, separate from Saran Wrap. HandiWrap begat Saran Cling Plus, and the original Saran Wrap begat Saran Original, which begat Saran Premium Wrap, which begat Saran Premium Wrap's Slide 'n Cut Bar®.

Whatever the genealogy, it's all plastic wrap, which means it's guaranteed to frustrate from the minute you take it out of the storage drawer.

You have a plate of supper leftovers to refrigerate. You reach for the wrap ...

Like its cousin, packaging tape, plastic wrap camouflages its most recent tear-off point quite effectively. Sometimes you can find it the same way you view the Pleiades in the night sky – by not looking directly at it. Whichever way you choose, the correct way is the one you did not choose.

The serrated metal cutting edge is sometimes attached to the lip of the lid, sometimes to the body of the box. It doesn't matter what part it's attached to; you will pull the plastic toward the part it's not attached to. This will cause the box to bend and make it even harder to get a clean tear. A clean tear is every wrap user's Holy Grail – and something they have about as much hope of finding.

It's a stretch, but let's assume that you get the plastic unrolling uniformly from one end of the roll to the other and actually achieve a clean tear. With a false sense of security, you think you're now holding enough plastic to seal the plate of leftovers.

Naturally, the first thing it does is cling to itself.

This is plastic wrap's signature shortcoming. Blame it on static electricity if you will, but I think there's a conscious, malevolent presence at work. No, not poltergeist. More like the Overlook Hotel in *The Shining*.

You manage to un-cling it.

You cover the plate, only to find that its diameter is larger than the width of the wrap.

Because of that, the wrap doesn't cling to a degree that would justify the use of "cling" as an action verb. Certainly not as tenaciously as it always seems to want to cling to itself. At this point, you're tempted to buy Saran Cling Plus on the mistaken assumption that it will give you the cling you need.

Don't. "Cling Plus" is an alias.

The ideal is a seal airtight enough you can bounce a dime off the plastic, but on a normal-sized dinner plate, as you've proven, this is geometrically impossible. The next best remedy is to tear off a second length of wrap and place it over the dish perpendicular to the first. That piece clings even less tightly than the first, because it is being asked to cling to its own kind, and there is a biblical injunction against that sort of thing.

The sad consequence is that your plate of leftovers enters the refrigerator disheveled. Hope that your mother-in-law is not around to witness this.

Perhaps you've noticed on the supermarket shelves the latest in plastic wrap dispensing, Saran Premium Wrap's Slide 'n Cut Bar®.

"Maybe I should give it a try," you say to yourself. "Maybe replacing the serrated metal edge with a couple of pieces of plastic really is the answer."

Don't be hard on yourself for thinking that way. That's what I thought, too, and, initially, things were going as the box promised me they would: no more dispensing hassles.

Then one day, the slide piece of the Slide 'n Cut Bar disappeared, leaving me with a No Slide 'n No Cut Bar.

I was forced to use kitchen shears.

And how did that go? Picture the coastline of Norway.

A few days and a new box of plastic wrap later, the missing slide reappeared from under a utility table when I was sweeping the kitchen floor. My son told me the Slide 'n Cut technology had so frustrated his sister that she'd sent the piece flying across the room.

And so the torch – or at least the urge to torch – has been passed to a new generation of plastic wrap users. Long may they suffer, as their forebears have suffered, even back unto four generations.

How essential is this week's column? Why, even writing it is a less essential chore than the least essential of the least essential chores listed.

The Least Essential Chore Contest

It takes a special kind of homemaker to distinguish the truly purposeless from the merely tedious. That's why I'm sure you'll agree that the top entries in the first annual Least Essential Chore Contest have really hit the nail on the head, which, by the way, placed a respectable sixth in the Most Essential Chore Contest.

Contestants were asked to submit a totally pointless household task, accompanied by a brief, one-sentence comment justifying their entries.

Greg Groutgrime, a college senior and member of the Kappa Zeta Jones fraternity at the University of Pittsburgh, submitted "Refilling the Jet-Dry dispenser." Greg wrote, "It was a toss-up between that and *locating* the Jet-Dry dispenser, and anyway, doesn't the blue circle mean the battery's okay?"

"Vacuuming the basement steps," wrote Kyle Spreadsheetz, a 28-year-old slacker who still lives with his parents and plays his Nintendo Wii six hours a day in – where else? – the basement. "That's what the door's there for," says Kyle.

"Scrubbing the mineral deposits off the shower head," said filtration expert Maya Deltalady. According to Maya, "You can fix that problem by installing a water-softening tank or moving."

Lynn Kenmore-Sauers, fulltime at-home mother of six and about at the end of her housekeeping rope, submitted "Folding the underwear" shortly before leaping, panty-less, from the west rim of the Grand Canyon on her first vacation in 20 years. Her supporting statement, "Tell them I'm ..." was ruled sufficient to qualify her despite the fact that it was not a complete sentence.

"Writing your most frequently dialed numbers on that piece of paper in the wall phone," said Yao Ming, the 7'6" All-Star center for the Houston

Rockets. "I can't read them that far away and they're always at a right angle to your line of sight anyway, not to mention that cell phones store numbers automatically, rendering that little piece of paper irrelevant," said the man whose English three years ago was limited to "Pass it to me I dunk."

"Aligning the print cartridge," wrote Carly Fiorina, former CEO of Hewlett-Packard. "We put that in the instructions as a joke."

Former school teacher and silver spoon owner Laura Bush nominated "flipping the mattress," and had this to say about it: "Now that they only put the puffy quilting on one side, it just wouldn't look right – not that I've ever had to personally flip a mattress in my life." The judges agreed that she'd been given accurate information about the puffy quilting.

"Fertilizing" was submitted by a consortium of men calling itself the "Mowing Riders of Suburbia." "Who needs work that makes more work?" asked the Riders. It was hard to argue with them.

Outside in the lobby, various malcontents whose entries were received past the deadline carried signs announcing their favorite least essential household task:

> "Saving your medical receipts"
> "Washing the washer tub"
> "Voting"

But in the end, the judges chose "removing the extra slats from the mini-blinds" as the absolute Least Essential Chore of all. The second place trophy, awarded posthumously, went to "folding the underwear," with "vacuuming the basement steps" edging out "aligning the print cartridge" for third.

The mini-blinds entry was sent in by a Miss Havisham, a recluse who claims she doesn't even know how to open hers. Of the slat-removal job, she wrote, "You have to be a real oddball to spend your time doing that."

And a few other things, Miss Havisham. A few other things.

Dog droppings and shrunken laundry are a homeowner's worst nightmare. If only that were so.

Lawn and Laundry

Being an admirer of successful niche businesses in a depressingly corporatized world, I have to hand it to Poopie Scoopers R-US.

Well, maybe not *hand* it – that's why I'd be hiring them in the first place.

I was filling my tank at a Wawa the other day when I saw their flyer pasted above the pump:

> Tired of cleaning up your dog's droppings?

Personally, it was the stomach contents I had trouble with. But I've yet to see a flyer offering *that* brand of cleanup. If my dog is any barometer, there's an untapped market for the Poopie Scoopers of the world if they're brave enough to tackle the upper as well as the lower end of your Shih-Tzu's digestive tract.

Tired? I suppose every pet owner tires now and then of cleaning up his pet's droppings. The question is: Is it worth $20 a week to shed yet another activity that used to fall under the category called "Daily Living?"

Poopie Scoopers R-US would like us to answer that in the affirmative. Their web site argues that "Demographics and social trends point to an accelerating demand for personal services for busy professionals and executives, single parent households, and people who simply have better things to do than scoop up after dogs."

Let's see, we already pay people to groom them and walk them, not to mention feed and play with them while we go away. If we abdicate our poop cleanup responsibilities, too, what are we left with?

Virtual Dog?

Does that then make us virtual dog owners?

Hey, we *all* have 'better things to do than scoop up after dogs. That's not the point.

The point is, what's going to be left of living if we farm it all out? It's as if the natural world has ceased to be integral to our lives. Already, someone else cuts our grass, mulches our beds, cleans our gutters, rakes our leaves, shovels our snow, cleans our houses, and prepares our meals. Meanwhile, we work and commute ungodly hours to earn enough money to pay for these services.

Sorry, scooping company, but I found my solution years ago to the discredited task of picking up after my dog: dry dog food and a half-acre yard. When I combined those ingredients with Mother Nature's formidable decomposing agents – wind, rain, and riding-mower tires – I could avoid canine stool harvesting altogether. And that freed me to devote my time instead to laundry. Specifically, all those bath towels, hoodies, and tee shirts that had landed in (or never left) my kids' hampers since the last week's wash.

There's nothing quite so deflating as noticing that the handful of darks you just transferred from the bottom of the hamper into the rising waters of the washing machine appears to have already been folded. It's like discovering an error on a spreadsheet: Calls the whole hamper into question.

If only I'd had someone back then to come in and handle the absurd task of re-laundering my kids' clean clothes for me. But with no entrepreneurs to answer my own "accelerating demand for personal services," I was left to my own devices. Deliciously, those devices included the power to shrink my kids' hoodies to the size of dog warmers.

Agitation-R-Me

So who knows? Maybe we *should* work more hours to pay for not having to do the work that keeps us from working more hours. We're evolving creatures, aren't we? On the other hand, maybe this complex behavior is evidence of some *intelligent design.*

I said maybe this complex behavior is evidence of some *intelligent design* ...

BEFORE THE CLOUD

Your username and password are incorrect.

And We Wonder Where the Time Goes?

6:15 pm: It starts out simply enough. Some online business to conduct with my health insurer. I've been slow getting around to it, but now I'm ready for action.

The Aetna phone rep tells me, "I'm going to email you the link to the website where you'll enter your information."

"Can you read me the link over the phone?"

"I'm going to email you the link."

"You can't just read it to me?"

"I'm going to email you the link ..."

An hour later, the link arrives.

"Whoa," I have to admit, "that's a pretty long link" (if you consider https://ips.aetna.com/Retail/Home_Login_Consumer.aspx?bid=5InVOC2cW54%3dwithaHeyNonnyNonnyandaHot-cha-cha a pretty long link).

I click on it and go to the Aetna website.

7:30 pm: Since I'm a first-time user, I enter my name in the "username" fields, create a password and confirm the password. The screen displays a message:

Your username and password are incorrect.

Relative to what?

I enter my email address for username and get the same message.

I try a different password.

I make my name the password and the password my name.

I put *e* before *i* in my last name in violation of the spelling rule.

Nothing works.

The phone rep's supposed to be working till 8 pm. I email him for help with my identity crisis. A multitasker like me can't sit idly waiting, so I go and do something productive: I turn on the Phillies game.

9:00 pm: no response. I call it quits for the night.

6:00 pm the next evening: I'm back, but, before I can get going, a popup tells me the antivirus program installed on the computer has expired. "Why wait until trouble strikes?" I figure, and I click "Renew."

Whadya know? The company is inducing me to upgrade to their 2006 version by charging me less than if I keep my old 2003 version.

I sign up, not thinking to ask, "Why would they do that?"

The 2006 program downloads, but, before letting me proceed, it tells me I have to uninstall the 2003 version first.

Simple enough. I'm a seasoned uninstaller.

I watch as the screen measures my progress: Twenty-five percent complete. Fifty percent. Seventy-five percent.

It stalls at 75%.

7:30 pm: Several minutes have gone by and still no movement.

I turn on the Phillies game.

A half-hour later, I check back. The screen hasn't changed. I minimize the uninstall window only to find that another, smaller window has been hiding behind it. This is like having the FedEx driver say to you, "I delivered your package three days ago and put it in the basement with your Christmas decorations."

There are items in Quarantine. Would you like to delete them?

You're @#&!!ing right I would.

As soon as I click the "@#&!!ing right" button, things get moving again faster than an unclogged toilet.

With 2003 now uninstalled, I successfully install the 2006 version.

In the time it takes for me to use the bathroom, the new antivirus program has taken it upon itself to begin a scan of the 120,000 or so files on the hard drive.

King Lear has a shorter running time.

In the interim, I knock off the Sunday *New York Times* crossword puzzle and watch a few episodes of *Law and Order*. When the scan is complete, I close the program, but, first, it has a message for me:

Refreshing. Please wait.

For some, "refreshing" is a water ice on a hot summer night. For others, a professional ballplayer who's not on steroids.

For me, "refreshing" means, "All this to save five bucks? You are such a dummy."

I wait while the program finishes refreshing. It never does. It is "not responding."

10:15 pm: My response to the "not responding" message is to go back to watching the Phillies.

They're not responding either.

Shouldn't there be messages on the TV screen for people like me?

"The Phillies are not responding."

Or, "Chase Utley is in Quarantine. Would you like to delete him?"

Back at the computer, I close the insidious "refreshing" window and return to the Aetna website.

You may remember the Aetna website from Chapter One.

"J. Shields?" I type, thinking, "Maybe if I add a question mark ..."

30

All this headache for a single consonant?

K, Too (Not the Mountain)

Can you remember the day you created your first username? It was a painless transaction – if your name was Mary, Queen of Scots.

Mine wasn't. Even though it was only the "Pope Benedict Ab Workout" web page I was visiting, my name was already taken. So was the combination of my first name and middle initial. First and middle initials crashed, too.

I was too principled to stick a numeral in there, and my confirmation name, Francis, never even occurred to me – which is how works with confirmation names. So I added my wife Kristine's initial, k, to my last name and lower cased it.

In connubial conjunction with the initial of my own name (which, for security reasons, I've led you to believe all this time is "John"), that did the trick. And isn't that how it should be between a husband and a wife – working together for a common goal?

Thus was born my user name. But you know how it goes. A few more websites and one day you think, "Maybe I should vary it up a bit." That's when we begin to need "the list," because we are naively certain we're going to remember those variations. And when all we had to remember were Norton and our bank, we did.

But soon, the screens on our desktops and laptops were teeming with names like Amazon, Monster, Amazon Monsters, Gmail and Pornhub.

My list? After trying to access a dozen or so sites by relying only on my memory and three user-name variations, I compiled them into one neat, typewritten page. It listed each site and the password and username needed to enter it. But as we have all discovered, there's no end to the list. Currently, I have at least another two dozen websites handwritten on the page, a page grown more precious to me than my children's birth certificates.

Some people are so paranoid about concealing their user-name-and-password list that they conceal it beyond recall. Not me. I need mine visible, and it is – right on the bulletin board behind me, along with the various words of wisdom I pin up there to keep me grounded. I'd have to say my favorite of those are by Samuel Beckett, of *Waiting for Godot* fame, whose craggy looks I'm hoping to possess when I'm 70.

"Yes, in my life, since we must call it so, there were three things, the inability to speak, the inability to be silent, and solitude, that's what I've had to make the best of."

And then something unexpected happened to me one day. My wife announced she was divorcing me – no small thanks to Beckett's "three things." To heal, I found it important to make a clean break with anything that reminded me of a past turned painful. It was a long process, but I finally undocked myself, save for one niggling detail: a certain lower-case "k."

To remove it, I'd have to visit over sixty websites that require me to enter my username. And to do what? To change my username.

Hmmm.

On second thought, I don't care how miserable my memories, or how haunting the ghosts of the past. For the k, I may have to make an exception.

CHEESES

Why is it always Jesus or his mother's face that people claim to see in the oddest places? How come it's never Steven Spielberg's or Lady Gaga's or Voltaire's or Meryl Streep's or ...

That Is a Crock, Madame

I've been thinking about what to get our kids for Christmas, and my job's just been made a little easier. I can go online and buy each of them a Virgin Mary Grilled Cheese Sandwich tee shirt from Golden Palace.com.

Maybe you've been following the story about the lady from Ft. Lauderdale, Diana Duyser, who made a grilled cheese sandwich for herself ten years ago, and after taking a bite, saw the face of the Virgin Mary on the bread. She put the sandwich in a clear plastic container with some cotton balls (standard sandwich preservation protocol) and left it on her nightstand. In all those years, she said, it never grew mold or crumbled. That, along with some hefty casino winnings that subsequently came her way, led her to conclude, "I do believe that this is the Virgin Mary Mother of God."

Recently she put the sandwich up for auction on eBay with the stipulation that "this item is not for consumption," and yesterday, Golden Palace.com, an online casino, bought it for $28,000. The company's CEO said, "We believe that everyone should be able to see it and learn of its mystical power for themselves."

We could end this column right there, and you could provide your own commentary. But I get paid to produce, so let's continue.

Every year, the religious significance of Christmas is buried deeper and deeper beneath mounds of crumpled wrapping paper. But now I can, with one modest purchase, help put the "Christ" – or at least His mother – back into Christmas. And for that I have Golden Palace.com and eBay to thank, not to mention Ms. Duyser herself, whose willingness to make money off ... er, part with ... her sacro-culinary creation made all this possible.

But beyond the spiritual benefits we can derive by adding that item to our carts, the story raises questions both profound and practical.

When Ms. Duyser says "this is the Virgin Mary Mother of God," it's not clear whether she believes it's the sandwich itself that is the Virgin Mary or just the likeness *on* the sandwich. This has tremendous theological implications. After all, heretics were tried and burned (or should I say grilled and toasted) over disputes about whether Christ was actually, or just symbolically, present in the Communion bread.

And where is the sandwich to be kept? The Shroud of Turin, believed to be Jesus's burial shroud, has its own reliquary (a place for holding reliqs) on the altar of the Turin Cathedral in Italy. How, one wonders, might Golden Palace.com choose to display and preserve the Virgin Mary Grilled Cheese Sandwich? This presents a dicey problem (heh heh) for a casino that exists only in cyberspace.

Do hits on a web site count as a pilgrimage?

And not to impugn Golden Palace's sincerity in wanting to share the "sacred sandwich" with the world, but might there not be another motive afoot? Can't you picture some flat-broke gambler hunched over his keyboard, down to his last roll of the cyberdice? He's looking for help, praying for his luck to change. Who will he turn to?

Golden Palace.com has the answer for him: Just click on this icon.

Psychologists attribute the grilled cheese sandwich phenomenon to our human instinct to look for and find patterns in random shapes. But for those of you trying to replicate the Blessed Mother at home in your kitchens, here's a little hint from the sandwich maker herself: She didn't use any butter or oil.

No wonder she had a visit from the Homemaker of homemakers. Who would even think of using oil to make a grilled cheese sandwich? That would be, to borrow from one enterprising tee-shirt maker, "sacrilicious."

I don't know, I thought I'd write about the Devil for a change.

Deviled Parmesan

Something – call it an omen – told me I should withhold this column until a later date, that if I didn't, further mishaps would befall me. I am only now making it public.

Today was June 6, 6/6/06, and the devil and his helper were behind the counter at the pizza restaurant when I walked in at precisely 6:06 and six seconds to place an order.

Rushing to a meeting, I'd debated whether I'd save more time by calling in an order to my usual pasta spot or by stopping somewhere else along the way.

I chose the latter. Or should I say the latter was chosen for me. (No, I shouldn't, because the passive voice is usually frowned upon.)

L'Inferno was a restaurant I'd never patronized. When I entered, the devil was making a fresh pie and didn't see me come in.

Or did he?

When he turned to face me, I ordered spaghetti with marinara sauce then inexplicably second-guessed myself and said, "Can you make that fra diavolo instead?"

A faint grin seemed to form at the corners of his mouth as he answered, "Sure. Why not? To go?"

"Yeah, to go, and a large Coke, too."

Satan then told me, "That'll be ten minutes."

On hearing that, I balked at placing my order, realizing I could've called ahead to *L'Erotica Ballerina de Polo*, where they knew me, and my order would be ready when I arrived.

The prince of darkness sensed my hesitancy and quickly changed his estimate. "Seven minutes. Maybe even six. Six. Sure, six minutes," he said. "I only say ten to cover my tail."

With that assurance, I consented to my food order and sat down to wait.

A pleasant, cooling breeze was blowing in through the restaurant's open front door. I used it to break the ice with the fellow who'd just taken my order, not knowing at the time that he was Lucifer.

"Man, that breeze feels great."

The devil didn't say a word. Maybe pleasantries and cool breezes weren't his thing.

As promised, my pasta order was ready to go precisely when he said it would be. The devil's disciple … helper, a teenager who'd been working the sandwich grill, wrapped my dinner order, and the salad that came with it, in separate paper bags.

I paid the helper. He handed me the bags and my large Coke. Meanwhile, Beelzebub said, "Thanks for being patient, my friend. It's a virtue." Was it my imagination or did he have a hot pepper on his tongue that seemed to make him spit that last word out?

No sooner did I get into my car than I noticed the paper bag containing the spaghetti fra diavolo seemed a little wet. I sat it on top of the bag containing the salad and drove off. Turning left at the intersection of Hell and Damnation … wait, what made me write that? It was Jarrett and Norristown. Anyway, as I was turning left, the bag with the pasta mysteriously slid off the salad bag. I propped it back immediately, but not soon enough to prevent several drops of grease from landing on my passenger seat.

They formed a strange pattern on the velour upholstery resembling three upside-down nines.

I cursed my misfortune and the teenage helper's inept packing job.

If I'd called *L'Erotica Ballerina*, I thought, this wouldn't have happened.

I made it to my destination on time, though, and without further leakage ... or so I thought. But when I lifted the bags from the passenger seat, there appeared a large, red sauce stain about six inches by six inches, approximately six inches from the edge of the seat.

And that's when it hit me.

No, not the numerological "coincidences." The large Coke.

Well, first it hit the side of the passenger seat while I was backing out of the car trying to carry the leaky paper bag. Then it hit *me*. What didn't land on my pants spilled onto the passenger seat in a pattern that looked suspiciously like a pair of cloven hooves.

Needless to say, my meal that night was a little on the dry side. On the bright side, however, I won't have to worry about this happening again for another hundred years, when advances in upholstery cleaners will have rendered the whole subject moot.

LANGUAGE

Gated community: *n. a development with a fence around it; a penitentiary.*
New Cynic Dictionary, 2007 Edition

Iamb Inspired

My inspiration this week is "Poet's Walk," a new, gated community of luxury estate homes under construction in Ivyland. Not long ago, I said of Poet's Walk, disdainfully, "Watch. The streets'll be named after poets, and two of them will be Dickinson and Wordsworth."

Well, I was wrong about that.

They're the models.

Historically, imaginative naming of tract-housing developments has never been a builder's strong suit, or even his aim. The paramount requirement for a development's name is that it suggests some combination of 1) the natural world 2) open space and 3) England. Horse references are an acceptable alternative.

A development whose name is "Someplace" *at* "Some Other Place" gets bonus points. The Ridings at Squires Meadow, for example, where square footage has replaced the apostrophe as an indicator of ownership.

Horse and England themes are old school now, but a peek in the Sunday new homes section shows the others holding strong.

The Fields at Creekview. Hearthstone at Woodfield.

Then there's Providence Crossing (where everyone stops for the Light).

To me, a name's a winner when its parts are interchangeable. "Excuse me, I'm trying to find Stonewood at Fieldhearth." "Oh, you must mean Fieldstone at Hearthwood. Mile ahead on your right."

Exclusivity has long been inferred in the names given to new construction; now, it's flat-out proclaimed. The Enclave at Millridge. The Reserve at Bally

Spring. The Estates at Ridgewood (not to be mistaken for The Ridgewood Estates in Atlantic County).

All in all, then, kudos to Poet's Walk for doing it a little differently.

The problem is that, out of all the poets they could have chosen from, the marketing people selected for their website an unlikely trio of non-materialistic *non*-poets to help sell their product.

That famous luxury-home owner from India, Mahatma Gandhi, for example: "Be the change you want to see in the world."

Then there's Henry David Thoreau, the *essayist* from that un-gated community known as Walden: "Go confidently in the direction of your dreams. Live the life you've imagined."

These are men I associate with civil disobedience, not million-dollar properties.

And then there's the French moralist, Joseph Joubert, unknown to millions, who contributed this to the Poet's Walk website: "Imagination is the eye of the soul." (Or some combination of the three.)

If imagination is the theme, then right now I'm imagining a well-worn path forking off from The Road Less Traveled (see the Frost model). It's worn with the footsteps of poets, and it leads to a bucolic, wooded setting, adjacent to a large meadow called The Ridings. From there, one sees fields with creeks and woodfields with no creeks, just wood. A mill sits on the ridge by a spring. It's called Spring Ridge Mill. Next to it stands a house, a house with a hearth made of stone. We could call it Hearthstone House. Let's. It is filled with pedestrians, poets, and pedestrian poets, who have walked there. Why? Because none of them could afford public transportation, let alone a mortgage.

Before I close, give me a chance to make up for my earlier, incorrect prediction about Poet's Walk with these new ones:

1. There will be no street named Plath's End.
2. You can forget about a Kahlil Gibran model.
3. The community will have no actual poets living or walking in it.

By the way, the other model plans are the Kipling, the Browning, and the Manchester.

The Manchester?
You got me.

Ambitious people angle like fly fishermen to obtain positions on boards of directors. Had they only known about . . .

SM Editors

It's a shortened deadline this week, so I've brought in a guest to do most of the writing. A little background, and then I'll turn it over to Katherina.

Back in April, on the recommendation of a colleague whose meds must have been mislabeled, I sent an email to a company named "SM Editors" that, in effect, said, *I am a man of superior copyediting skills in search of freelance editing opportunities. Have any? Thanks. Resume attached.*

Next day, I heard back from them:

> *Dear Mr. John Shields*
>
> *It will be a pleasure to keep your name on our Editorial Board. It is to inform you that as a Board Member of PROFESSional Editors & Writers, you would be please involved in the correspondent academic and promotional activities for the company. You may introduce the company within your circle and among your acquaintance.*
>
> *Best wishes for a long-lasting and productive collaboration.*
>
> *With kind regards,*
>
> *Thank you.*
> *Best regards*
> *Katherina Johnson*

PROFESSional Editors & Writers (Formerly called SM Group of Editors)

Talk about freelance editing opportunities! With two errors in the salutation alone, this response had me thinking that maybe it was actually a test that I was supposed to correct and return.

It was fairly obvious that the writer was someone for whom English was a second language, but, please, "Katherina Johnson?"

I never replied – I have standards, too, you know – and didn't hear again from PROFESSional Editors & Writers . . . until this week.

> Dear Dr. Shields,
>
> This is with regards to our previous correspondence regarding offering online, free-lance job of Editor, Reviewer, Writer, or Translator's under the banner of PROFESSional Editors & Writers.
>
> (Have oxygen ready.) It is a pleasure to offer ample opportunity to those who are keen to be an active part of the organization serving the best mutual interests. Recently, it has been offered a discounted complete publication package for authors of regular papers/books or publishers/organizations, which includes writing, language editing, scientific reviewing, formatting keeping prescribed guidelines, graphics' or chemical structures' development, graphics' or chemical structures' improvement for quality, tables' designing, layout or cover page designing (for books), designing & printing (books, flyers, brochures, Ads, press releases etc.(authors or publishers/organizations must chose at least four services at a time in order to be entitled for a discount of 25% off on the total service charges).
>
> "The website www.sm-editors.com," it continued, "is being updated for potential flaws and updates," an update refuted by the potential flaw that followed it: "Your name will soon be included on the board page."
>
> Thanks & regards,
> Katherina Johnson
> Co-coordinator
> PROFESSional Editors & Writers
> 1306 Preston Lake Drive
> Tucker Georgia GA 30084

(It's not just Monty Python that has a Department of Redundancy Department.)

As a board member and surprise holder of a terminal degree, I recognized my fiduciary responsibility to act in the company's best interests, so I penned the following reply:

> *Dear Katherina,*
>
> *Variant of Katrina, isn't it? And speaking of disasters . . .*
>
> *Do not – repeat, do not – put my name on your board page or anywhere else. In exchange, I promise I will not introduce the company among my acquaintance.*
>
> *Consider a career change.*
>
> *No thanks & ill regards,*
> *PROFESSor Shields*

After which, I stepped down from the board.

New expressions, or even old ones that have lain dormant, can materialize and spread overnight in our wired culture. People use them without really considering if they make sense.

Freedom of Mis-Expression

"Point your finger, and nine more point back at you."

I've been hearing that expression a lot lately. Before that, never. Even back to my womb days, when the closest thing to it I remember hearing was "as long as he has all ten fingers."

As with most faddish expressions in our pop culture, I'm not happy unless I'm criticizing it.

It's not the "point" it's trying to make that bothers me. After all, this is just another way of saying "Let those without sin cast the first stone," (which is how Jesus was always able to finagle Mary, His Mother, to the head of the line).

The problem with this finger-pointing expression is that it's anatomically impossible.

When I point my index finger, only three point back at me, and they don't so much point as curl. My thumb is the only digit aiming in the same general direction as my index finger. But even its role is a supporting one, like an understudy to the lead, and less about directing attention than about firming up the entire operation.

If I point with both hands, I can get up to six fingers moving in my direction, but that's the maximum – from these hands anyway.

Some people are born with extra fingers – like Antonio Alfonseca, who was a reliever for the Phillies. Maybe it's different for people like him. ("Point your finger and any number from ten to twelve point back at you.") I do know this: his digital surplus didn't help his earned run average. If anything, it inspired among spectators another hand gesture known, also erroneously, as "giving the finger."

On the other hand (oof!), there was a famous pitcher for the Chicago Cubs a century ago, Mordecai Brown, whose nickname was "Three Fingers." (I like it when nicknames need no explanation.) The fingers on old Mordecai's pitching hand ... well, put it this way: if it wasn't bent, it was missing. But it made him a very effective pitcher, proving once again that less is more.

I blame the Internet for malaprop expressions like this finger-pointing one. Someone latches on to a line and it spreads like a jaded prostitute.

There's another making the rounds that's driving me absolutely nails-on-a-blackboard bonkers: throwing someone under the bus.

Look, I know buses. I grew up in the city. Neither of my parents drove, so I rode buses everywhere. Here's what happens: The bus stops at a street corner, at a place the locals call the "bus stop." There, it picks up and discharges passengers. Then it accelerates – I use the term loosely – as it pulls away from the bus stop. Half a city block later, by the time it reaches its peak speed of four miles an hour, it's time for it to slow down as it approaches the next bus stop.

Is that the kind of motor vehicle action that strikes you as capable of hurting anybody?

There are two logical fallacies here. First, when would you have your best shot at throwing someone under the bus? When it's stopped. But how's that going to be effective? Second, when individuals are thrown into contact with a bus for the purpose of eliminating them, it's usually a) in *front* of the bus and b) in movies. But I think I've proven beyond all doubt that a moving bus, unless it's taking seniors to the Atlantic City casinos, isn't traveling fast enough to hurt a pointing finger, let alone an entire human being.

If you really want to do someone in, you can't beat a train. SEPTA Regional Rail, Amtrak Acela, the subway (express, not local). Any of those will get it done for you far more efficiently than a bus. You just stand there on the station platform with your "trainee," and when one of those babies comes flying by, a little hip action and ... bingo!

But the bus metaphor isn't so much about premeditated murder as it is about saving one's own hide. And ironically, most of those who use the expression don't take buses themselves. So, I propose we get rid of the expression altogether and go back to "throwing them to the wolves," which worked just fine before buses came along and was environmentally tidier.

*Where seldom for nerds / an encouraging word /
And the hardest / are on / Saturday*

Cross Words for the Crossword

I've never met Byron Walden but if I ever do, I'll knock him ACROSS his head with a "earthen building block" (5 letters) then pour "volcanic emission" (4 letters) DOWN his trousers.

Byron Walden, my "donkey relative" (3 letters)! Any idiot knows "Byron Walden" is just a "false name" (9 letters) for "English Romantic poet and Concord pond."

Whatever his real name – and I'm suspecting it's an anagram of Byron Walden – he (she?) has been my undoing.

For the past couple of years, doing the Sunday *New York Times* crossword puzzle has been an integral part of my Sunday routine. And my Monday routine, and my Tuesday routine. I'm proud of my ability to regularly solve it in its entirety – in pen. So proud, in fact, that I've even modified my resume:

EMPLOYMENT HISTORY:

2005-present   I regularly solve the Sunday *New York Times* crossword puzzle in its entirety in pen.

As with any task, the learning curve flattens the more you do it. The puns, the abbreviations, the maddening two- and three-word answers, all reveal themselves a little more readily when you know what to look for.

That's why the crossword "Byron Walden" created for the April 15th issue was so unexpectedly brutal. So malevolently sadistic. So preposterously "can't be done" (8 letters).

The puzzle's theme was "In Other Words." In each of the four corners was a pair of intersecting, 8-letter anagrams, for example, B-E-I-N-G-F-A-T and F-A-N-G-B-I-T-E. These letters, rearranged a third time, became yet another anagram, F-B-I-A-G-E-N-T, that was part of a separate, longer answer, a familiar phrase reinforcing the "hidden" theme of "In Other Words:" U-N-D-E-R-C-O-V-E-R-F-B-I-A-G-E-N-T.

There were four of these suckers, one for each pair of anagrams.

More torturous still was the fact that the only "clues" for these longer answers were the location of the other two anagrams. In the above example, "23-Across or 19-Down?"

As if that weren't challenging enough, solving the four sets of anagrams was like having to scale Lhotse and Nuptse to get to Everest. The surrounding words' clues were deviously misleading. Here are a few examples:

"Something that goes for a quarter" (9 letters). Answer: "Trimester."

"It begins here" (5 letters). Answer: "Aitch."

And the one that set me back two days:

"Words before roof and flag" (8 letters). My answer: "Raise the."

Correct answer: "Under one."

It took my plugging away off and on for nine days, but I managed to solve every clue except two: "Some toll units" (5 letters; answer: "Axles") and "Salt agreement" (3 letters; answer: "Aye").

In hindsight, those two look relatively simple.

That's why hindsight is "perfect vision" (12 letters).

You may be familiar with the expression "Pyrrhic victory." It's a reference to the Hellenic king Pyrrhus, who won two battles against the Romans but lost so many troops doing so that he is famously quoted, "Another such victory and I shall be ruined." A Pyrrhic victory, then, is one that leaves the winner in devastating shape.

In this case, me.

I've faced down many a clever puzzle creator and emerged victorious, but you, Byron Walden (Ronald Newby? Waldo R. Benny? Len B. Anyword?

Wo, Bryn Laden!), you have exacted a price for my success that makes a pound of flesh look like the portions you get at Subway these days.

Brain dead, that's what I am now. Brain dead. D-E-B-A-D-R-A-I-N that's fallen on me ever since I threw in the towel on "Some toll units." A-D-I-R-E-B-A-N-D playing "The Alphabet Song" in my head over and over.

I'm sapped. No longer do I look forward to curling up on my recliner with the latest Sunday *Times* crossword spread across my lap desk in all its empty-squared glory. No more the thrill of the hunt. Just the pitiful whimpering that emanates from the core of a beaten man.

Time for something different. Time for tamer stuff. "Can be done" (6 letters) stuff.

Maybe the Middle East. Maybe world hunger.

"Anagrams," a ram sang.

(Author's note: "Byron Walden" is a real person. Math professor at Santa Clara University.)

Answers:

Earthen building block – brick
Volcanic emission – lava
Donkey relative – ass
False name – pseudonym
Can't be done – undoable
Perfect vision – twentytwenty
Can be done – doable

Now that we've gone global, our ever-changing language is ever changing faster than ever.

Of Greek Philosophers and Jalapenos

By my brain's calendar, it was about a year ago when chipotle first appeared. Maybe it arrived while I was trying to track down what "tapas" meant and I missed it. All I know is one day it wasn't there and the next it was everywhere.

I get thrown off my game when a new word appears whose meaning I'm clueless about. Don't get me wrong, there's something exciting about that. But it also makes me paranoid. Everyone else knows what it means but me.

"Ululate" is one of those words. "Boffin" is another. And now "chipotle."

As both a word and an entity, chipotle is an utterly unnecessary addition to my life, its existence immaterial to me except insofar as I can get a column out of it. I'm long past varying my consumption patterns simply because of a new word on the menu.

Take "Jagermeister," for example. I hear it mentioned with enthusiasm and cachet among mostly younger drinkers, and it obviously refers to one Mister Jager, whoever he is. (I know enough to know that it's not Mister Mick Jagger.) But because a Bloody Mary and a gin-and-tonic mark the boundaries of my liquor forays, I couldn't tell you *what* a Jagermeister is, only that, when you're hammered, pronouncing it becomes, in effect, a sobriety test. ("Police report says you called it 'Gajersteimer,' son.")

But something else makes chipotle problematic. Ululate and boffin I could at least pronounce (maybe not ululate). Even jagermeister (when I'm sober) is no phonetic speed bump for me. But chipotle ...

Bottle ... Aristotle ... chipotle, right?

No, not right. And that's what makes it wrong. It doesn't sound anything like Aristotle, or coddle, or throttle. But it should. It should sound like Aristotle, at least, because it's SPELLED LIKE THAT!

Worse, the word has *multiple* pronunciations. It can either be chi-pot-ly, like "motley," or chi –poat-ly, like "remotely." Or, the last syllable can sound like "-lay," thus doubling the ways we can pronounce it.

No word should get off this easy.

Well now that I've brought up the subject, I guess I should share what I've learned about chipotle. It's a smoke-dried type of jalapeno chili pepper, most of which are produced in the northern Mexican state of Chihuahua. (That's *chee-who-uh-who-uh*, after the grotesque dog of the same name). Because the drying process removes most of the moisture, it takes ten pounds of jalapenos to make one pound of chipotle. (In ancient Greece, Aristoatlay had the brain power of ten ordinary Greeks combined. Unlike jalapenos, however, he was never smoke-dried – except once in Macedonia, punitively, when he erroneously taught his pupil Alexander that Asia Minor was a musical term.)

Our culture craves novelty the way cacti crave the desert. When chipotle becomes passé, there will be another chipotle to talk about, to claim status through, to provide our lazy, entertain-me minds and eroding interpersonal skills with another fad to fleetingly engage each other with. A new wrinkle to be out in front on until the next latest thing comes along.

It's unlikely that that new wrinkle will be Aristotle. But if it is, just ask someone this rhetorical question: What assures the adequacy of our explicandum and the possibility of synthetic *a priori* knowledge if not the analytic character of all implication relations upon which correct deductive inference must be based?

That'll burn your tongue better than any hot pepper I've tasted.

POETRY I

Fran may be a poet, but that doesn't mean I can't send him a few couplets of advice now and then.

Poetry the Easy Way

My friend Fran is a poet. He's been at his craft for years, but only this year did he finally gain some local acclaim when he read his work at the Philadelphia Fringe Festival. With titles like *The Death Door, Dead Rabbit in the Yard,* and *Good Friday and Rain,* you can understand his difficulty in building a following. Building a mausoleum, maybe.

I'm pretty sure there's a better path for Fran to take, and that the Philadelphia Fringe Festival is, by definition, not exactly the road to renown in the poetry world. But what makes *me* so qualified to make that assessment, you ask? What can *I* possibly know about entrée into the poetry pantheon?

Well, it just so happens that *I* have credentials. And here's how I acquired them:

I was exploring an educators' job-search website one day when a popup ad for the "International Library of Poetry" asked me if I wanted to learn my poetry IQ. Who wouldn't? Eleven questions later, I learned that I was at a level at which people like me are considered "among the most talented of poetic artists."

So, there's that. But my qualifications go far beyond that.

Clearly, the probing questions I fielded on rhyme scheme, alliteration, and free verse could reveal only my general poetic knowledge. If I wanted a personalized assessment of my "creative potential and poetic flair," (oh, and a shot at a $1,000 prize for best poem) I needed to write an original poem for evaluation by a judging panel.

I like making connections between things, so, given that I'd already digressed from my job search to address the pressing concern "What is my poetry IQ?" I chose Adult Attention-Deficit Disorder as my theme and set to work.

Twenty enjoyable minutes later I had a finished product. I clicked "Submit" and whisked it off to determine my creative potential and poetic flair.

A week later, I received a letter announcing that *I Am a Dad with Adult A.D.D.* had made it to the semifinals of the International Open Poetry Contest, an accomplishment that AUTOMATICALLY QUALIFIED me to advance to the final competition.

I liked that rule and plan to lobby for it for my high school baseball team.

But think for a moment about the magnitude of my achievement. Rainer Maria Rilke, the German poet who never made it to the semifinals of anything, needed ten years of quiet and a few uninterrupted days of inspired mystical experience in a castle in Switzerland to compose the *Duino Elegies*. Yet my 20-minute burst of iambic pentameter and penetrating introspection (Is there any other kind?) had vaulted me from base camp to the near pinnacle of international poetry with one mouse click.

Who said writing's tough?

What's more, the Selection Committee wanted to publish my poem *on its own page* in a "classic, coffee-table quality hardbound volume printed in two colors on fine-milled paper specifically selected to last for generations."

Takes your breath away, doesn't it?

And that wasn't all! My poem was to appear in what promises to be one of the most highly regarded collections of poetry the International Library of Poetry has ever produced: *Eternal Portraits*.

Straight to the finals, *Eternal Portraits*, fine-milled paper … Fran, you've been going about this the wrong way, pal. Don't you think you're missing the boat here with your Fringe Festival offerings? I'm sunning on a cruise ship deck chair somewhere in the Caribbean while you're dropping anchor on a tugboat in the East River.

Eternal Portraits. A "superb collection of over 200 poems on every topic." Every topic, Fran.

Do you need more convincing? Well, what if I told you that *Eternal Portraits* is just the latest in a series of "highly sought-after volumes" that include *Tranquil Rains of Summer, Star Dust in the Morning,* and the unforgettable *Verdant Lands of Spring.*

Oh, and lest anyone think the selection of *I Am A Dad With Adult A.D.D.* was motivated by commercial considerations, I have it in writing that it was on the basis of my "unique talent and artistic vision."

By the way, I'm available to help aspiring poets chart the waters of their own poetic fortunes (for a modest stipend). I also do titles, and I've submitted one I thought up, *Forever Mildew,* for next year's highly sought-after volume. If it's rejected, I have *How Much Can a Grecian Urn?* polished and ready to go.

SPECIAL DELIVERER

Next-day hernia delivery.

Being Santa's Helper Has Its UPS and Downs

The late George Plimpton gained fame by trying out various occupations for which he was ill-suited and then writing about his experience. Professional football, boxing, and trapeze-flying, among others. Among contemporary writers, David Sedaris, perhaps ideally suited, made his name recounting his travails as an elf at Macy's Santa display.

There is precedent, then, for writers making fools of themselves, as I did last week, when I signed on as a seasonal driver helper for UPS.

The job description said, "This a very physical outdoor position working in all weather conditions and variable temperatures with continual walking and lifting of packages that typically weigh 25-35 lbs. and may weigh up to 70 lbs."

How bad could it be?

"We can give you work right on up to December 23rd," said Rob, the delivery coordinator.

"Great," I answered. I could do anything for two weeks.

The next day, it snowed. An icy snow.

I rendezvoused with my driver, a seasoned, by-the-book fellow named Tom, who was filling in for another driver that day. Tom showed me how to use his real-time tracking gadget but, basically, my job was to run packages from the truck to the house and then run back to the truck.

Notice I said "run."

After a couple hours of this, I was building up an appetite. "What time do we break for lunch, Tom?" I asked.

He offered me a Fig Newton bar.

There was ice everywhere. To avoid slipping, or at least cushion the fall, I would often avoid the driveway and bound across the snow-covered front lawn to make my delivery at the front door. I'd give a few loud knocks on the door before retracing my steps back to the truck.

By the time I got home that night, we had made 95 stops and my knuckles looked like breasts.

But I didn't fall once, and I finished my day tired and sore, but ready for more.

Day Two: Same temperature, same driver, different route. The plan: We'll do the businesses first and save the residential neighborhood for the end of the day. Sounds like a good idea to me.

About midday, I take my first fall on some ice, landing on my left side. I check my left wrist to make sure the titanium plate holding my radius together is still doing its job. I check my neck to make sure I haven't herniated any new disks. (I am – have I mentioned – pushing 55.) I look back at the truck. Tom has not seen me go down, so I don't even mention it when I climb back in. Instead, I strike up a conversation about workers' compensation for seasonal help.

UPS regulations require that seat belts be used at all times while driving. Twisting left to pull mine on, twisting right to take it off, pulling the door open, pushing the door closed … falling out of the truck would be less painful.

Shortly after my fall on the ice, I'm running through the snow on one particularly long front lawn when my boot simply rips in two. The bottom detaches from the top from my heel all the way to the ball of my foot.

I still have three more hours of deliveries to make.

We arrive at the residential neighborhood. I'm now running through snow on a shoe that has no instep support.

To me, "neighborhood" means people living in relatively close proximity to one another. The houses in this "neighborhood" have driveways the length of the George Washington Bridge. Several of them could support a triple chairlift.

In many instances, leaving the package by the garage is my path of least resistance, since the path from the driveway to the front door is unshoveled. But Tom is of the "right way" school of parcel service, so I deliver to the front door. With my throbbing knuckles from yesterday's deliveries pleading, "Please don't knock," I try instead to send happy thoughts to the homeowners that their packages have arrived.

From a standpoint of time and footing, my best bet is to avoid the driveway and pavement and instead take the grueling hypotenuse from the truck to the front door – via the snow-covered lawn. I notice I am not bounding today as lightly as the day before. My boot is gobbling snow like Pac-Man. And I'm beginning to question the cardiological wisdom of leaving the neighborhood for last.

This is when my knee, the one without the cartilage, begins asking me, "What were you thinking when you filled out that W-4?"

The residential neighborhood might well have been called "Bataan." Near the end, I make a hundred-yard mistake: I deliver to the wrong house.

Next morning, when the UPS coordinator calls, I tell him, "I cannot do snow today. My boot tore apart yesterday, and I simply will not run across lawns."

"Today's the big day, John," he tells me.

With seven more business days until Christmas, I'm wondering what makes this day the big day?

I am paired with Don, a driver in Sellersville. I bring a spare pair of shoes but wind up not needing them because most of my deliveries are to modest residences of human scale with shoveled paths. We make 160 stops but, surprisingly, I'm feeling okay. At the larger properties, my driver is reasonable about the garage vs. front door issue, and I don't fall once. It has been a good day. That evening, I tell my son that I think I'm over the hump in adjusting to the physical demands.

Next morning, however, I'm assigned to Dave, whose route is mostly businesses. His truck is packed to the gills, and it's three hours before we can clear the aisle of boxes and create a path to the rear door. We're off-loading large numbers of heavy boxes and bulk items. Delivering to a bakery, I bounce off the concrete when I trip on a step.

Later, I ask Dave, who's been driving for 15 years, "Dave, how long does it take for your body to acclimate to all the running and lifting?" (I omit "falling.")

"It never does," he says. "I'm sore every day."

Oh, boy.

It's dusk, and a fresh snow is falling as we prepare to deliver to a development of townhouses. The homes are wonderfully close to the street and to each other. This is fortuitous, because by now I am barely ambulatory.

The next morning, UPS tells me they're going to pair me with Dave again because we worked so well together.

Meanwhile, I can't walk from one side of my nightstand to the other.

It's time to throw in the towel.

Unfortunately, I cannot throw the towel.

Would you mind throwing the towel for me? Please. I've been Santa's helper long enough.

Okay, UPS. Let's get our priorities straight.

FedEx's Secret Weapon

Last week, I got a call from UPS asking me if I'd re-up as a driver's helper for the busy Christmas season.

This is like America asking Donald Rumsfeld back as Secretary of Defense.

Not that I wasn't hard-working and earnest. It was just that, with my middle-aged knees and Medicare eligibility, I wasn't the right man for the job.

You may recall my four days of hell as a seasonal UPS driver's helper a year ago. It was manual labor's version of David Sedaris's Christmas gig as an elf at Macy's. Only, he lasted longer, got lunch breaks, and was probably a perfect fit for the job.

After I handed back my official UPS brown jacket and slacks to personnel with a contrite but embarrassing "No mas," I felt that I'd let down the entire company. That my absence would sabotage delivery schedules from here to San Francisco. That drivers would tape my picture on their sun visors, hoping to spot me crossing the street in front of their trucks. "Didja hear about the wuss that bailed on Charlie?" they'd be saying.

Apparently, UPS didn't see it that way.

The voice on the line practically caroled the invitation to me to come back to my old job. For UPS's sake, I was hoping its stockholders weren't aware this was happening.

My initial impulse was to say are you crazy? It's a year later and I'm *still* hobbling. But then I figured if UPS wants me again, they must really be desperate. Maybe I can leverage that desperation to my advantage. You know, get a few on-the-job concessions.

So I decided to see what kind of deal I could make for myself. I began with a request for a morning cup of hot latte waiting for me when I boarded the truck. Consider it done, they said.

"I refuse to climb over packages again," I said. Last year, the truck was so crammed with packages from floor to ceiling that it took the first five hours just to create a path from the cab to the rear door. I insisted the aisle be clear from the start, with the added guarantee that I would not be required to offload sets of tires or, for that matter, any package heavier than a Nintendo Wii.

UPS said they'd make the driver do those things, while I sat up front sipping my latte.

Next I put limits on the size of driveways I'd have to traverse. Any longer than 30 feet or with a slope greater than ten degrees, the driver had to transport me to the garage door. I was surprised when they yielded on that point.

The absence of a lunchbreak last year was a personal hardship. Sorry, but peanut butter crackers between stops doesn't cut it for this driver's helper. This year, UPS has agreed that, if I consent to return, my driver will drop me off at the nearest Taco Bell and come back for me 45 minutes later (a compromise we reached when I couldn't get them to agree on a full hour).

For most of the year, packages are on-loaded so that the address sequence generally conforms to the driver's route. But during the holidays, with seasonal help hired to handle the volume, the loading process gets a little more unreliable and chaotic.

Not on my truck, I insisted. I wanted every item loaded in the correct sequence. "And remember what we agreed about keeping the center aisle clear."

"We'll see what we can do, Mr. Shields."

"That's not good enough," I replied.

They teleconferenced with the CEO, Mike Eskew. Not a problem, Mike assured me.

Last Christmas season, I had to drive several miles each morning to a designated location and meet my driver there.

"Pick me up at my door," I insisted.

We had to iron out some details about whether I'd report on days when it snowed or the temperature fell below 50 degrees (I wouldn't) and about my refusal to wear those unflattering brown shorts. Oh, and about that mechanical lift I wanted installed so I could get on and off the truck more easily.

In the end, I got everything I asked for. I start back this Friday, the 22nd. Then I'm off for the weekend, and the next day is Christmas, which is a holiday. UPS told me they wouldn't need me after that. Good thing, too. I'll need a break by then.

FINDINGS I

Harper's "Findings" may be on the back page, but in my book it's on the top shelf.

Exploding Ink and Tipsy Monkeys

We're living in the wrong country. Check out these goings on in the U.K. (source: *Harper's Magazine* "Findings," June & July, 2006):

- A British inventor unveiled a three-wheel vehicle that gets 8,000 miles to the gallon.
- A British chicken named Freaky underwent a spontaneous sex change.
- A giant rabbit was rampaging through vegetable gardens in northern England.

Now *there's* a country that looks like it's having itself some fun.

I became a *Harper's* reader by accident. One of those school magazine drives was rearing its ugly subscription head, and I was compelled to do my part so that my son John could earn "Dress-Down Friday." Could the stakes have been greater?

I found the articles intellectually stimulating and philosophically to my liking, which meant I could finish one of them before the next month's issue landed in my mailbox.

The "Findings" page has become my favorite part of the magazine. It's a compilation of what its title says it is, findings, from various investigative fields. All are real, the product of actual research and news gathering. There is no commentary, just a matter-of-fact presentation using simple declarative sentences with an understatement that can be laugh-out-loud funny.

The end result is a fascinating monthly briefing on what we're learning about – and doing to – ourselves and our world.

For instance, *"British scientists* (those Brits again) *claimed that men drink heavily at sporting events in order to compensate for their masculine shortcomings."* (In Philadelphia, it's to compensate for the masculine shortcomings of the athletes they're paying to watch.)

Or this: *"Researchers identified the gene that controls whether people have wet or dry earwax."* (I'm willing to bet that whatever kind you have, you didn't know that there even *was* another kind.)

Or how about this one: *"The FDA approved a skin patch for delivering drugs to hyperactive children; the patch will carry a label warning that such drugs have been linked to heart problems, psychotic behavior, and hallucinations involving worms, snakes, and insects."* (I'd rather remain a hyperactive child, wouldn't you?)

And on they go. (Me, too.)

- *Rhesus macaque monkeys drink more alcohol when they drink alone.* (As opposed to tying one on with the boys at the Rh Factor Lounge.)
- *Two cloned mules failed to win a race against normal mules.* (But did the cloned mules finish in a tie?)
- *An Australian inventor received a patent for a vomit ejector.* (This has generated some interest among Rhesus macaque monkeys.)
- *Researchers in Texas discovered the genes that cause birth.* (Now, can they reverse engineer the ones belonging to Texas politicians?)

And finally ...

- *A patent was issued for exploding ink.* (But every time they go to print it out...)

All these findings have implications. The fun, or the depressing part, is in trying to figure out what those implications are.

In any event, people in China reportedly are eating fewer owls.

FAMILY

There's a special corner in Heaven for the hamsters, goldfish and finches we buy for our children to teach them "responsibility."

Mac, Our Finch

Before we started having kids, my wife and I owned a zebra finch that we named Mac, because his chirp sounded like the number pads on the early money-access machines – or MACs, as they were called. When Johnny was 7, we gave him his own zebra finch for Christmas. He liked our "Mac" story so much that he decided to keep the name.

We were realists about expecting a 7-year-old to be on top of the responsibilities of pet ownership, and we fully anticipated working as a family unit on Mac's upkeep. Just like we shared the load with Chloe's hamster Furball, who ended up looking like a cross between a Molokai leper and Nosferatu before we were through with him.

Still, as pet-keepers went, we weren't nearly as bad as our neighbors the D'Arcys. They killed two hamsters in under two weeks, for an average of better than a hamster a week.

Mrs. D'Arcy struck first when she chose Clorox as her cage-cleaning agent against what proved to be the intuitively sound protests of her 6-year-old daughter. That eliminated hamster number one. A few days later, one of the rambunctious D'Arcy boys reacted to a finger nip by flinging the replacement hamster over his shoulder like a bride's garter at a wedding reception. The surprised little life form flew until it met the wall and plunged to the floor like the down elevator in the Tower of Terror.

"Damn hamster," the young D'Arcy offered, sounding like a dyslexic reading a map of Holland.

So, no, we weren't as bad as that, but … well … you be the judge. These tips on caring for zebra finches are from *exoticpets.com*, a website that, like the D'Arcy hamsters, is no longer with us:

- *All finches are social and should be kept in pairs.* (As I said, his name was Mac.)
- *Finches do not crave social interaction with people so, unlike parrots, do not need to be in a busy social part of the home.* (That's why we kept him the kitchen.)
- *Any cage should be easy to clean.* (Which is different from saying it should be* kept *clean.)
- *Make sure the cage is not so cluttered that the finch cannot fly back and forth. Keep an open flight path through the length of the cage.* (Bor…ing.)
- *Provide fresh drinking water daily.* (Does God provide outdoor birds with fresh drinking water daily? Totally unrealistic.)
- *Food dishes can be placed on the floor, though not under perches, of course.* (Of course…)
- *Again, these need to be cleaned daily.* (But what does "daily" mean exactly?)
- *A shallow dish of water should be provided several times a week for bathing.* (Whereas a deeper one can last indefinitely.)
- *Feed a good-quality seed mix, although this should never be the sole diet of your finches.* (We offered him sole once. He didn't care for it.)
- *Check that the seeds are fresh by sprouting them.* (We preferred an atmosphere of trust.)
- *A variety of greens should be provided.* (Does the chlorine residue from the old water count?)

As you can infer, we didn't always do right by Mac, who died this weekend an old, old bird of 10. Especially in the aftermath of the divorce, when he got lost in the shuffle.

We knew he was near the end, but I didn't want him to pass untended, so I brought him over to my house for a few days. Cleaned his cage. Set him in front of windows with nice shade and the best breezes. Even left him and the cage outside in the yard for stretches of time.

He'd never been outdoors. I felt tempted to open the cage door and release him, his final moments spent doing what he was born to do. But he was so old I couldn't do it. It was *my* vision talking, not his. His cage was home to him. Like a prison lifer, he couldn't make it anyplace else.

I picked him up a last time and trimmed his claws. Held him gently and stroked him. Let him nip at my finger. He squirmed away briefly for one last flight but didn't get far.

By now, his once-excited chirp had faded to a couple of monosyllables, when he could summon any voice at all. Mostly he'd sleep in the privacy he'd made for himself beneath the paper towels at the bottom of the cage.

I'd have kept him with me, but I brought him back to Kris's house instead, for one reason only: so my cat wouldn't get him.

Mac died that evening, in the place where a family broke up. I don't think he was too thrilled with being returned to that place. That's my spin on it anyway.

In the end, given how her world had been upended, my daughter's graduation by a hair proved her, if not an honors student, then at least a student with honor. Her principal, on the other hand ...

Chloe Graduates

My daughter Chloe has been the subject of a column or two in the past nine months, and, no, I'm not writing now to announce that she's given birth.

In those earlier pieces, I was tongue-in-cheek about her efforts to obtain a driver's license and deadly serious about her academic suspension and dismissal from the basketball team for admitting to having some pot with her on the team's trip to Florida,

Since that incident, and because of it – and because of the dissolution of her parents' marriage – her road to graduation has not been a smooth one. Anything but. For the past six months, I've felt like a moviegoer who can't look, for fear of what's going to happen next.

So, it's with a profound sense of relief that I share with you the good news that my daughter graduated from high school tonight. I witnessed it with my own eyes. Saw the diploma change hands myself.

At the moment it left the principal's and entered Chloe's, I'm told I began spouting a stream of Gaelic and Chilean football cheers and dancing the Suni dervish dance – which got me escorted from the auditorium, but not before the Hatboro-Horsham Educational Foundation booked me for their 2006 concert series.

One thing disappointed me, though. I'd expected at least a fleeting acknowledgement from the principal for pointing out to him back in January that a nine-day, out-of-school academic suspension in a block-schedule school like his was equivalent to an 18-day, out-of-school suspension in a school with a traditional schedule. If that's not relating math to the real world, I don't know what is. But he was too busy at the podium delivering his speech, a speech, oddly enough, made up *entirely* of U2 song lyrics.

Everywhere I looked there were parents I knew. Parents I hadn't seen since I coached their kids in soccer and Little League a decade ago, parents from the basketball team, parents from those endless musical rehearsals in elementary and middle school. All those familiar faces. Like having the last thirteen years of your life pass before you.

It felt as if every back-to-school night we ever attended had been compressed into one big room on one evening.

Conversations were fleeting because there was always someone else to shake hands with or hug. Not all the news was good, though. The goalie on my girls' U-10 soccer team, whose dad coached with me, was hospitalized for severe anxiety disorders that lasted her entire senior year. Another girl, also the daughter of a guy who coaches with me and a 3.9 student in her own right, had self-esteem issues and so hated every day of her four years there that she turned down membership in the school's National Honor Society.

Add in Chloe and here are three girls who had a common denominator in their disordered lives: I was their head coach.

As the ceremony got under way, the principal introduced the first of the two co-valedictorians by name, and she gave an insightful speech about missed opportunities for seeing the humanity in one another. After she finished, the other co-valedictorian stepped to the podium, but the principal, who was perhaps still enthralled by his recent channeling of Bono, never bothered to introduce her. She was followed by the class salutatorian, and, again, I'm sure I speak for all in attendance that we were thankful to have a program to read so we could learn who he was. I began thinking that maybe the principal's iPod was the problem.

Hello, hello / I'm at a place called Vertigo.

By this time, regardless of what was going on inside the principal's head, inside mine was the voice of Father Ryan, my wise, old, sophomore Latin teacher, noting, "Shouldn't the salutatorian have gone first?"

When my daughter first started at this high school, I suggested to a faculty member that Latin should be included in the curriculum.

But I still / haven't found / what I'm looking for.

In the end, what does it matter anyway? For Chloe, it's all behind her now, and tomorrow is a new day.

Farewell and hail.

Brace yourself.

Teeth Wisdom

If you are a parent of children under the age of 11, thank me for what I'm about to tell you: 1) Nothing in the parenthood manual says orthodontist appointments for your children are compulsory, and 2) the Constitution does not guarantee the right to perfectly straight teeth.

If only someone had told me those things 12 years ago.

I had lunch last week with my beautiful daughter Chloe. During one of her smiles, I noticed that the tooth between her upper right canine and her two front teeth had moved slightly behind.

For those who don't speak Orthodontese, that means her teeth aren't straight anymore. After three grand and three years – three just grand years – her teeth aren't straight anymore.

The simple explanation is that she didn't get her wisdom teeth extracted and now they're growing in and crowding the other teeth.

But I know the real reason: After she got her braces off, I didn't make sure she wore her retainers every day and night for the next five years.

Bad father. Bad.

People who don't have kids or who have never worn braces don't understand that the day the braces come off is the beginning, not the end, of your troubles. Not that it's easy being a parent of kids in braces. The monthly appointments you have to drive them to forever. The liquid you have to remind them to swish around in their mouths each day so they don't end up with permanent white stripes across their teeth. It's no party.

But, once the braces are in, at least you don't have to worry about keeping them in.

Now retainers...

A kid is going to find ways not to wear them, he's going to lie and say he wore them, and then, he's going to lose them. Or step on them. Who wouldn't? He just spent three years with a mouthful of metal that he can't remove, and now he's being told by the orthodontist that he'll have to wear his retainers day and night for another six months and every day after that until his first child's Confirmation?

Right.

On whom, then, does the burden of policing this preposterous directive fall?

Here's a hint: not the kid.

I would rather *pay* a retainer than make sure my kid is wearing his. It is, in my opinion, the single most degrading task a parent has to do. And all because the orthodontist has convinced you that not wearing the retainers will undo all the results you just paid good money to achieve.

I bought into that once, with my oldest child. The result? Just what a son wants to see in his father: an anal, Gestapo she-male.

I know what I'm talking about. As the at-home parent for ten years, I was Orthodontics Central for all three of my kids. Appointment scheduler, school notifier, driver. It grows old fast, and at some point you begin to question the saneness of it.

It wasn't as if my kids' teeth made people want to drop some change in their lunchboxes. One had a little overbite, another had a space – God forbid! – between his front teeth, and Chloe, well, I still don't know what was wrong with *her* teeth.

More to the point, it wasn't as if each was begging, "Daddy, please get me braces."

But a mouthful of beautifully aligned teeth, well, it's their birthright, isn't it?

No, it's not.

Then why do we do it?

Good question. What did it get Chloe, except those permanent white stripes on her front teeth?

It's too late for me, but maybe it's time to rethink this rite of passage that bonds both parent and child in a form of what we might call "dentured servitude."

Better, maybe, to put the money to other uses, like in an interest-bearing instrument for the child to use when she's an adult and can decide for herself the relative merits of perfect teeth.

A Father's Day reflection.

By Definition ... My Dad

Dictionaries are like houses: They grow old with you, and you don't own many of them in the course of your life. When I was growing up, we had an unabridged one that my parents had been given as a wedding present. Along with your standard four million words, it contained colorful representations of various flora and fauna.

It's hard to imagine a dictionary scaring you, but one page in particular terrified me. It depicted an enormous, fanged rattler and conjured images in my head of an illustration I'd seen in *The Swiss Family Robinson*, in which a boa constrictor is coiled around a distressed donkey, squeezing the life out of it.

Maybe that's why, in my early twenties, I had the inspired idea to give my father a new dictionary for Christmas. When he opened my present and saw the spanking new *Random House Dictionary of the English Language, the Unabridged Edition*, he seemed genuinely moved.

I wasn't sure he could abandon his old one, though.

John Shields Sr., my father, was not what you would call a forward-looking or imaginative man. When, as a boy, it was time for him to choose his Confirmation name, he selected the same name as had been given him at Baptism. Consequently, his full name was John Joseph Joseph Shields.

Ever one to stick with the tried and true, he ate Total cereal for breakfast and brown-bagged an American cheese sandwich to work every day for twelve years.

So you can infer that here was a man of routine, for whom change held little appeal.

Living on my own, I didn't have much opportunity to follow Dad's progress with his new word finder, but when I'd visit my parents for dinner, I'd notice its presence in the living room – a good sign.

The famed concert pianist Artur Rubenstein was notorious for his ability to perform brilliantly despite his self-proclaimed disregard for practice. He attributed this phenomenon to "the two greatest gifts a person can possess – a good memory and self-confidence." My father possessed the former in abundance, but something stifled the latter.

And so he settled for a 35-year "career" with the Post Office, sorting mail. But he knew by heart the names and zip codes of every avenue and side street in the city of Philadelphia.

I never used a zip code directory for my Christmas cards. Using Dad was faster.

After my father died, I was sorting through his belongings, and I rediscovered the dictionary I'd given him. Its page edges were blackened with the printer's ink that had transferred onto his hands from the newspaper he read every day. (There have been major advances toward eliminating the annoying transfer properties of printer's ink. Unfortunately for the newspaper industry, they were followed in short order by another major advance called "the Internet.")

I use a dictionary, too. It's a habit I've acquired. I have my own, but in an emotional moment of remembering, and on occasions like this one – Father's Day – I'll use his.

It's almost like touching him. The ink from his hands is distributed along the outside edges in a bell curve -- heavier toward the middle, lighter at the extremes. This tells me he liked to open to the middle then work his way forward or backward to the word he was looking up. That, or most of his curiosity fell between letters "G" through "T."

One thing for sure: there was no spelling deficiency in the man. He won a loving cup as an eighth grader in a citywide spelling bee – an example of Rubenstein's assessment of a good memory as being one of life's greatest gifts.

In most every other way and for various reasons, I've consciously tried to be *un*like my father. But I'm proud to emulate his practice of using the dictionary. And I don't mind adding that, like him, I, too, can spell so well you'd think I chose "Webster" for *my* Confirmation name.

The "Wilson" phenomenon: Can we love inanimate objects?

A Friend for All Seasons Is Gone

Everybody remembers Wilson, right? The volleyball that became Tom Hanks' buddy in the film *Cast Away*. Hanks' marooned character, Chuck Noland, discovered it when it washed ashore after the crash of his FedEx cargo plane. The ball was a Wilson brand, so that's what Noland, in his growing need for social interaction of any kind, named it.

I suspect we all have a Wilson in our lives, some inanimate object that, for whatever reason, comes to mean the world to us. A first car. A baseball glove. A waffle maker, who knows? What differentiates an object like Wilson from these other examples, though, is its role in keeping us alive. Without Wilson, Chuck Noland doesn't survive.

My "Wilson" is my weekly pill organizer, the compartmentalized rectangular prism of a pal that's been with me for close to twenty years, almost from the day I had to begin taking daily immune-suppressive medication for my kidney transplant.

Faced with a slew of assorted pills, I learned early on that uncapping and re-capping medicine bottles and peeling seals from the corners daily wasn't gonna cut it. I'd known about these things called "pill organizers," or "pill reminders," because I'd bought one for my father a few years earlier.

Being a twice-a-day organizer, his was more complex in its design than mine. Its flip-open lids ensured that the evening pills could only be accessed after the morning ones had been taken. But there was nothing preventing someone, i.e., Dad, from taking the evening doses immediately after swallowing the morning's, or the next day's on the same day as the current day's.

I learned this first hand when he took a header onto the asphalt while getting off a bus, and an emergency room blood test found him to be toxically overdosed on his epilepsy medicine.

Dad died a few months after that episode. Among his personal belongings that I kept was his pill organizer. An ironic attachment, as it turned out, because a year later I was diagnosed with the early symptoms of kidney failure, condemning me, too, to a lifetime of pill organizing.

Pill holders are for old people, right? But there I was, at 38, with one of my very own. Mine was my sturdy companion for a third of my life, longer than any pet I've had and almost as long as my marriage. It sat passively on the kitchen countertop, simplifying my life and marking my days as a transplant recipient with the same daily regularity as my razor and toothbrush, only with far greater urgency.

I confess I took its presence for granted more often than not.

And then one day it was gone. Uncharacteristically, I had failed to keep track of it on a trip away from home, and when I was unpacking upon my return, I saw that it had not returned with me. No dramatic drifting away on the current of a lonesome ocean, like Wilson. Just a mundane, left-behind oversight.

Unlike the Hanks character in the movie, I never gave my blue, plastic little guy a name. Like him, though, I mourned this inanimate helpmate's passing. I prepared the following brief eulogy for a memorial service attended only by me:

"My pill organizer was an object of few words. Stolid? Yes. Phlegmatic? Undoubtedly. But always there for me when I needed it. It took life one day at a time – S, M, T, W, T, F, S – and never felt compelled to make more of any day than it already was. "Th" or "Sa," for example. Sure, it flipped its lid once a day, that I'll concede, but not of its own accord and, hey, don't we all?

"May it continue providing its invaluable service to some prescription-inundated soul in South Carolina."

Of course, pill organization remains mandated for me, so I got on with my life and bought a replacement. Twenty years later, and the only design advance I can discern is larger daily compartments. We can debate whether that represents a true "advance." What is not debatable is that I've lost a true pal.

The tasks have fallen to me. Which ones? All the ones that used to belong to my parents.

Tending the Headstone

Yesterday would've been my father's 90th birthday. It wasn't until I was looking at the dates on the headstone that I realized that. I don't visit my parents' grave very often. Just on an as-needed basis. I guess that sounds cold. Some people visit their family's graves regularly on holidays and on anniversaries of their loved ones' births and deaths. That seems a little too locked into the past, but maybe it's more than that. Life is hard, and we find our comfort where we may.

Every so often, I have an urge to talk to my mom and dad, and when I do, I'm grateful to have this place to come to. Whether it's the headstone, or the uneven, grassy ground beneath my feet, or the majestic blue spruce at the end of the row that I count on to orient me to their gravesite, all impart a tangible sense of connectedness. I wonder how people in our mobile society find that connectedness when they're living halfway across the country. To have a place to come to is a good thing.

One time, I had our children accompany me, because that six feet of dirt beneath their feet is the closest they'll ever get to my parents. My mother and my father died before our first child was born, and I cannot describe the size and shape of the hole *that* divine timetable has left in my heart.

That this most recent cemetery visit of mine turned out to be such a milestone date uplifted me. Dad's 90th. Not that he ever got close; he died at 69. But for reasons having to do with frozen moments in time and our own mortality, we humans enjoy noting how old the deceased would have been were he/she still alive. "John Lennon would have been 64 this year," or, "If Marilyn Monroe were alive, she'd be 80."

In the twenty years since my father died, all the older-generation relatives have passed away, leaving only me. The gravesite is mine to tend to now, a task I deemed to be only for the old when I was younger and more self-absorbed. It's a role one is never anxious to assume. But something compels. Family. A longing.

So I take closer note of the headstone than ever before. There's not much to do there, but if not me, who? Mostly it needs some fresh dirt and seeding around its base to cover the exposed, unhewn concrete that anchors it to the ground, ground that was disrupted for the final time in 2001 with the burial there of my dad's sister Genevieve.

The headstone stands back-to-back with one from the next row. They're about six or seven inches apart. (No wasted space in cemeteries.) My family's stone is unpolished, and its back, deprived of direct sunlight by its larger neighbor, is mottled with green. I examine half a dozen or so nearby stones to see if they share these features. But every one of them is polished and green free. I grin at these examples of Shields family thrift but cherish the simplicity and the humble roots they represent.

Buried there are my paternal grandparents William and Sarah, my parents John and Margaret, my aforementioned aunt Genevieve, and the site's mysterious first occupant, one Anna Gallagher, whose identity and relationship to me and my kin are unknown. No telling how old she'd have been if she were still alive, because the year of her birth was never engraved. (My ancestral tightfistedness at work again? "Well, you could go with only one date. That would save you a few bucks.")

Fifty years of wind and rain, frost and thaw have exacted subtle, begrudging concessions from the stone. The effects of the elements are evident in the softer lines of my grandparents' engraved names and dates, their letters and numbers a little wider than those of my mother and father. Less crisp.

I converse awhile with my parents, wordlessly covering a range of topics. Before leaving, I make a note to mark my calendar for a bag of topsoil and some grass seed come spring, and I wonder if I can scrub that green off, or even should. In this new and unfamiliar role, I am visited by the thought that those who never quite find their place find solace in tending to others.

LOCALS

The highlight of the annual New Hope Winter Festival is its Chili Cook-off, where several area fooderies submit their entries for judgment by epicures and prominent locals, including, this year, one who was neither – me.

Maya Mole

To my left, three chefs. To my right, three veteran Chili Cook-off judges. In the spirit of the event, I'll call them "seasoned." We are here to judge the ten entries in the Winter Festival's ever-popular Chili Cook-off.

The gentleman to my immediate left is Chef Earl Arrowood. Chef Earl is a culinary educator and certified chef d'cuisine (which, in English, means "chef of cuisine"). I'm hoping to learn from him if real chefs prefer "kyoolinary" or "cullinary," but the event organizers announce it's time to begin judging.

It's a blind tasting, with the contestants known to us only by letters of the alphabet. The categories include Overall Taste, Robustness, Consistency, and Spice Palatability. Creative Use of Ingredients serves as a tiebreaker.

"Where's Blowtorch Flamethrower?" I ask no one in particular.

Chef Earl had commented in the newspaper that every judge may have his or her unique system for evaluating, but, ultimately, all should agree on what tastes best. Now I really feel pressured – not only to have a discriminating palate but also a unique system.

There's nothing unique about my approach. Typically, I use the basic Yum/Yuk taste scale first developed by Grog in 12,800 B.C. But I sense that, for this occasion, I am going to have to raise my level of gastronomic sophistication.

I quick down a pint of lager.

The first entry is delivered to the judges' table. I taste. I smack my lips. I inhale the aroma. I study the texture. Meanwhile, while I'm still deciding on a score for the first category, Chef Earl has already finished grading his paper and set it face down.

"Why couldn't he have set it face up?" I think, as the makings of my own unique system begins to suggest itself to me.

The next chili is a chocolate mole (pronounced **chock**-lit **mo**-lay). I tell you this as if I know what a mole is, never recognizing it as part of "guacamole" because there it's pronounced like the "moly" in "holy moly." Well, pronounced by *me* anyway.

This chocolate mole tells me we're not in Kansas anymore. Teotihuacan maybe, but not Kansas. It has an intriguing, robust taste, with a lingering spiciness. That said, I'm more Cadbury than Cuernevaca when it comes to chocolate.

I'm getting into the flow now, nearly keeping pace with Earl. The entries are delivered to us at a steady clip that precludes small talk, and there's no comparing scores among the judges. Just the seven of us, silently tasting away, assigning our ratings, turning them in.

The variety, complexity, and *flavor* of the various chili creations is amazing, with ingredients like jalapeno, cilantro, venison, buffalo, and pulled beef brisket. Not to mention the moles and beans. During a momentary lull, Chef Earl expounds that the use of beans as an ingredient is "a Northeast thing."

"Northeast Philly?" I almost blurt out, before a timely belch intervenes.

After the last entry is judged, a few of us compare notes. Turns out we have a number of picks in common. Maybe Earl is on to something when he says we should all agree on what tastes best.

When the winners are announced, I feel a measure of self-satisfaction. Two of the three winners in both the Judges and the People's Choice categories are ones I rated highly.

And whadya know? The festival's organizers asked me to be a judge again at next year's cook-off.

Other than that, they did a great job.

Between 2004 and 2006, the Delaware River flooded its banks three times, inflicting significant damage on the arts and tourist communities of New Hope, PA and Lambertville, NJ.

The Delaware Deluge Sympathy Card

Flooding is no laughing matter, especially when it's happened to New Hope, PA three times now in 21 months. But humor can be a vital resource in emergency-management situations. Just ask FEMA or the White House.

In that spirit, I have composed the following form letter for present and, it would seem, future use by those wishing to send expressions of sympathy and support to the New Hope community.

The beauty of this letter is that it frees its recipient from having to read and be inundated by (eww, bad choice of words) every word of every sympathy note. The result: more free time to learn how to use that new generator or re-carpet the family room.

A second benefit: It can be tailored to any community and any natural or man-made catastrophe. ("Dear Greenlander, I was sorry to read about the melting of your icecap …")

I would retain 50% of the royalties from the sale of the letter. The other half would go toward the purchase of a water-sucking behemoth to be christened the "New Hope Really Big Sump Pump.")

> Dear [*name of water-damaged community member*],
>
> I was sorry to read about the flooding of [*enter applicable date*].
>
> The *a) indomitable, b) ebbing, c) overflowing* spirit of New Hope and its Main Street businesses is again being put to the test. I hope the *a) evacuation, b) squeegeeing, c) mildew mitigation* is successful and helps minimize the *a) stench, b) increased insurance premiums,*

c) suicidal ideations that a) may, b) will most certainly, c) always seem(s) to result.

What you've experienced in the past two years is a) of Job-like proportions, b) what happens when developers pave over the Poconos, c) just a taste of what's to come, d) all of the above.

Keep your a) sense of humor, b) chin up, c) head above the water. Things could be worse. You could be living in a) Baghdad, b) New Orleans.

You and your fellow New Hopeans are a) in my thoughts, b) storm troopers, c) too close to the river. If things get worse, though, you might think about a) bailing, b) breaststroke lessons, c) Arizona.

a) Sincerely, b) Swimmingly, c) Hydrostatically yours,

[Your name]

Easily Philadelphia's most hated bureaucracies, they are ...

The Philadelphia Parking Authority and Its Co-conspirator, the Bureau of Administrative Adjudication.

PPA and BAA. Think of them as a "pa and ba" shop. No, don't think of them as a pa and ba shop, because then you'll get all warm and fuzzy about them and you shouldn't, because they're villainous.

In brief, they rolled me for a $301 phony violation for "parking in a handicapped space." I'm still looking for their grounds, let alone an actual parking ticket. Substituting for the invisible ticket was a notification I received in the mail a month later.

Their methods down at Gotcha Central are coldly efficient. The PPA ticket issuer fabricates a ticket and the BAA rubber stamps "guilty" when you drag your sorry ass on down there to appeal. Simple as that.

You can appeal the BAA's first guilty decision, but all that'll get you is a second guilty decision. That's because the PPA delights in flaunting the term "prima facie" at you, a bit of Latin legalese meaning "You can't touch us." If a ticket was issued, says the PPA, you must be guilty. In other words, the burden of proof is on you, the ticketee.

Good luck with that.

Heading this satanic, mind-bending operation is Mr. Vince Fenerty, who's been with the Philadelphia Parking Authority for 28 years.

Make of that what you will.

Now, I'm not (entirely) impugning Mr. Fenerty's integrity here, but if you're writing a movie script or a novel and you need a name that connotes dirty deals, illegality and corruption, "Vince" is the one for you.

My sons' names are Nicholas and John. They mean "victory of the people" and "God's gracious gift." Vince, on the other hand, suggests "I'll beat the shit out of you." Oddly, Vince derives from the same Latin root as "victory" does, yet we equate Victors with nerds, while Vince suggests a prison sentence. Why is that?

But I digress.

Having made a strong case that Mr. Fenerty's first name has "payoff" written all over it, let's examine that surname of his: "Fenerty." Like his first name, it spells nothing but trouble. Here's why:

As some of you aficionados of obscure words and slow-moving water know, a "fen" is a swamp. A mire. A bog. And "inert" means motionless. Leaving us with "Fenerty," meaning "having the qualities of a stagnant swamp," "an inert quagmire," or, put another way, the Philadelphia Parking Authority, over which Vince reigns like a bayou bull alligator.

After my second appeal had been denied, I grasped the futility – and the $184 cost – of filing a third appeal with the Court of Common Pleas. My only choice was whether I would pay the $301 ticket in a lump sum or over a 12-month period.

I chose the lump sum to avoid seeing "Philadelphia Parking Authority" on my VISA statement for the next year.

But to savor a little payback, I mailed the check via certified mail directly to Vince Fenerty. I included a note describing to him how PPA/BAA had screwed me over. I told him he had his own choice to make: do the dishonorable thing and hand the check to one of his minions for cashing, or do the honorable thing and wipe it off the books. Choose the honorable path and he gets my word of honor to give his agency the kind of positive feedback it typically doesn't get or deserve. Choose the dishonorable path and he gets this essay.

A month passed and the check remained uncashed. I began to think of Vince Fenerty more as a potable stream than a swamp, a refreshing human being possessed of that quality we call "ethics." Then one day, I got a letter from the PPA telling me I owed the $301 plus a $55 penalty. I could picture Vince at his administrator's desk, gloating. "A choice? I'll show him who's got a fuckin' choice."

So now I'm fighting the $55 penalty. My case is currently "being looked into." The guy looking into it is named Corleone. That puts me in a handicapped space for sure.

To be an online dater, you have to learn to tune out phrases like "I'm living life to the fullest" and "not looking for any drama." Dating sites are filled with self-descriptions like those, ironically both empty and comic, but the discriminating searcher's patience will be rewarded. Mine was.

Is It Possible I've Found My Soul Mate?

Things are finally starting to look up for me romantically. I recently found a very appealing female on the online dating site I've been using:

PainfullyLongWalksOnTheBeach.com.

In her photo, she's sitting on the edge of a hotel room bed, big smile, legs crossed, and naked from her navel down.

Her screen name is "Asian Milf," but "Asian" covers a lot of territory, so to narrow it down, I'm going to say "Oriental." (I know the term's no longer acceptable, but there's a reason Agatha Christie didn't call it *Murder on the Pacific Rim Express*.)

As for "Milf," that's one I can't quite nail. I'd like to, though. Sounds Dutch to me.

I've been working on what to say in my first message to my potential soul mate. Here's what I've written so far, and tell me what you think.

Hello, Asian Milf,

I'm a john, er, John, and I was taken by the brevity and directness of both your profile and your outfit. You set the tone immediately when you declared, "I have a sweet tooth for chocolate – no other flavors need apply."

That will make it easier for me to decide what to get you for Valentine's Day.

Some of us on this site tend to list several things we're "really good at," but you kept your list to a single item: "Kicking the asses of White boys who insist on pissing me off."

Can you elaborate on that, A.M.? What do they do to get on your wrong side? Is your wrong side better than your right side? I can assure you that, while I am a White boy myself, I would never dream of testing your self-defense skills by irritating you.

No, there won't be any friction between you and me, I can assure you. I'd rather devote more of our dating time to shared pursuits, such as our mutual love of the British Broadcasting Corporation.

This is what attracted me to you, A.M. Your passion for British television is as uncompromising as your chocolate craving. When asked "the six things I could never do without," most people would reply with the obvious, like family, health, and long walks on the beach. But you wrote:

BBC
BBC
BBC
BBC
BBC
and oh yeah, BBC.

I have to ask, though, why didn't you call it "*the* BBC," the way most people do? Your way reminded me of those three-letter abbreviations you see in personal dating ads. No big deal, though. I know what you meant, and that's what counts.

What's your favourite programme, then? (Did you notice I used the British spelling? Hope that didn't piss you off.) I'll bet it's Masterpiece Theatre. Either that, or BBC World News. You seem the cultured, worldly type who likes to keep a breast on things.

Hey, thinking about it – oh, this is embarrassing! – I just realized I may have been completely misreading your list, and what you really mean by BBC is "Big Box of Chocolates." I didn't even consider that possibility. You and your chocolates! You're insatiable, Asian Milf.

Listen, my bottomless beauty, whether it's quality TV programming, chocolates, you name it ... I'm really interested in meeting you. You're one of a kind. Most women on this site who complete the statement "Looking for *blank*" say "guys who like girls."

Not many say "everybody."

DOCTORING

In this corner, a nun.

Shot Flu and Flu

I had my strategy for this year's flu shot all lined up. It was based on the chaotic, long waits that have resulted from the vaccine's scarcity. I pictured myself standing in a long, gray line of senior citizens, a line that would've been moving slowly regardless of how quickly the shots were being administered. And the odds of the shots being administered quickly weren't very good. Nurses repeating instructions, sleeves being rolled up by arthritic fingers, the difficulty in finding a muscle to inject into ...

The line would be made up overwhelmingly of women, because they outlive men. I would be in that line because my organ transplant status puts me in the high-risk pool of recipients.

Since I'm neither elderly nor patient, I needed a strategy going in to ensure that things would go quickly for me, because standing in line for five hours with 500 octogenarians was not in my plans for the week. So, being a male, and a young one relatively speaking, I had envisioned a series of conversations in the waiting line that would go something like this:

"Agatha? Why, what a beautiful name. I'll bet you had many gentlemen callers in your day. That many? Well, no surprise there. How could they resist those eyes, that smile? Me? Well, Agatha, I came here to flirt with pretty women like yourself. Ha, ha. No, actually, I have a kidney transplant. That's right, I can get very ill if I catch the flu. What's that, sweetheart? Yes, this line *is* quite long. Oh, Agatha, I couldn't do that. You've been waiting patiently. What's that you say? Well, if you insist. You're so kind. Oh, did you? A boyfriend who looked just like me? Why, Agatha, are you flirting with me? You know, I think this lady in front of me looks familiar. Can you excuse me while I talk with her a minute?"

But things didn't happen as I'd envisioned.

My actual flu shot experience felt more like a drug deal than a public health exercise.

A friend teaches at an area high school, and he told me I could come there for my shot and receive it with the teachers. He was apparently able to clear this with school personnel because of my provable high-risk status. I jumped on his offer. When I arrived at 7:45 a.m., however, my friend told me that there had been a glitch and that the nurse who was administering the flu shots had been allocated only 15 doses.

We tore through the halls, dodging students, and got to the nurse in time for me to receive the last available dose.

In the time it took me to do the paperwork and pay $20 (cash only), four or five others arrived. While the nurse was injecting me with the last of the precious preventative, they were milling about, looking perplexed. At least two of them were elderly. One was a nun. The others looked like teachers. All of them were out of luck. As for me, instead of feeling fortunate to have gotten the vaccine, I felt shame and guilt. The flu itself could not have felt worse. (Well ...)

This, then, is the current, sorry state of affairs: the elderly and chronically ill roaming the region like Christmas shoppers for Tickle Me Elmo dolls, in search of a vaccine that's vital to their health and damn near impossible to get.

The Bush Administration says two million more doses will soon be available, but two million is a drop in the bucket, and "soon be available" means three months from now.

Meanwhile, the Food and Drug Administration stated that officials are looking "throughout the world" for additional vaccine. So far they have heard from the Yanonamo Indians in the Amazon, who are willing to chip in with seven doses, and a private sector firm, Laden & Zawahiri Advanced Biological Solutions, which claims to have 200 million doses that it is willing to *donate*. The firm's CEO, Mr. O.B. Laden, says he can guarantee shipment on or before Election Day. Bush administration officials are said to be exploring the offer because it would represent a significant cost savings to the taxpayer over the $100 a pop the Yanonamo are charging in their primitive attempt at price gouging.

I envy people who can breathe unimpeded. When your lungs are happy, all the world's a hot-air balloon and you're its bright colors.

My Standard Deviation

In my informal polling over the years, I've discovered that deviated septa are more common than you'd think – and I don't mean our regional transit system (SEPTA, for my out-of-town reader). Although …

For those of you who are either undeviated or unfamiliar with the term, a septum (*plural* septa) is "a partition between two chambers." (Another term for it is "dissepiment," which I've never heard of, but to complain about a "deviated dissepiment" is to invite accusations of elitism and calls from general contractors.)

In people who breathe – and, for a finite time, in those who have breathed their last – the septum is the dividing wall between the nasal passages. When it's deviated, it's not straight. There's a very specific term for this: "crooked."

This is not a desirable alignment because it affects the amount of oxygen one can inhale through the nares.

(*Author's note:* I apologize for the vocabulary-building direction this piece is taking.)

To reiterate, and just so we're clear on this before forging ahead: My deviated dissepiment is compromising the quantity of oxygen available to me through my nares.

And you know what that means.

We'll get back to septa and their role in deviation in a minute. But first, in the service of building this column, I need to introduce a metaphor for living that you're all familiar with, this favorite adage from the sports world: "It's a game of inches." Or its variant, "It's a game of inches, Dan" (or the first name of whichever other male broadcaster is in the booth).

It's an expression used to illustrate that the difference between victory and defeat, success and failure, Pike's Peak and Pike's Penultimate Step is often a matter of miniscule distances. Horses win "by a nose." Sprinters by a hair. The putt stops rolling at the lip of the cup.

The world of medicine, both real and the TV kind, has taken the phrase and made it its own.

"If the bullet had been a quarter-inch to the left, he'd be a dead man by now."

"Half a centimeter closer and she's paralyzed for life."

In my case it's "If your septum were just a little less deviated, we wouldn't be talking about surgery." Not that I *need* surgery. But I often wonder what it'd be like to give my right lung a fighting chance in life.

And then there's the matter of colds.

Immune-suppressed people like me quake at the thought of a cold. You can imagine what happens to us when it's a reality. I'm now in week six, and the dearth of drying, healing air to my bronchi caused by my crooked dissepiment has begun to catch the attention of the local bacteria, who are anxious to please their bigger, more powerful, lung-dwelling neighbors, the Pneumonias.

Sometimes I can fight through the bacterial brown-nosing, but with colds like this one, all the Mucinex and Tylenol Severe Cold in the world, isn't going to be enough. No, colds like this one call for ... the Breathe Right strips. Their patented spring mechanism opens my right air passage j...u...s...t   e...n...o...u...g...h for air to get through. I can't tell you how wonderful and novel this feels.

Times like this, I'm wearing a Breathe Right strip 24/7. Eventually, the ends pull loose from my nose, and it looks as if an anorexic, flesh-colored butterfly has alighted there. That's when I have to stick on a new strip to minimize the public ridicule.

Soon, though, I'll have to go it alone again. One of these days, the last strip will come off, a sign that I'm out of the woods – or out of strips. And even though I won't have wise asses sticking my nose in their business anymore, I'll still be sad. Hypoxia will do that to you.

So, should I have surgery for something I've lived with most of my life? I hesitate, but then I hear the voices. One's coming from a broadcasting booth, the other from an operating room.

"It's a game of inches, Harry," says the one.

"Another two millimeters and it's a new life," says the other.

To put it another way, see what it's like when you have a little skin in the game.

Take My Epidermis ... Please!

On learning I have a kidney transplant, people often ask, "How are you doing with it?" My standard answer, because it's the truth, is "The kidney's fine. It's the rest of me that's going south."

It's gotten to the point where, if I'm not having surgery, it feels as if something's missing in my life.

Dermatological issues are my staple. That's because mutations from the medicine I take to suppress my immune system tend to show up in the body's faster-reproducing cells, such as skin cells.

I see my dermatologist four times a year, minimum. He and I like to talk baseball, and that's how we pass the time while he performs a full-body skin check on me.

"I like Utley batting second," he'll say, followed by "Hmm."

After the skin check's done, the routine goes like this: First, he tells me he's found some small, pre-cancerous areas on my face. These are my payoff for a lifetime of sun exposure. And what's neat is, because of my medication, I get to collect the dividends on them about 20 years sooner than I would've normally.

Next, he freezes them with his pressurized spray canister of dry ice.

Pss, pss ... pss, pss, pss, ... pssssss ... pss, pss.

To which I answer, "Ouch, ouch ... ouch, ouch, ouch ... ooouuuch ... ouch, ouch."

While my wince is still unwincing, he then mentions a mole or area of skin that is suspicious-looking only to him and the office biller.

"I'd like to biopsy that one."

I could refuse, I suppose, but things that are pre-cancerous in transplant recipients can lose that prefix faster than Tom Cruise can lose his sanity. And if they're cancerous to begin with, they progress so quickly that this is definitely not the time to show your doctor who's boss.

Over the years, my skin doc has mined all the easy-to-reach parts of my body. Now he's moved his "Silence of the Lambs" act to the middle of my back, between the shoulder blades.

After he takes his tissue samples, he sends me home with instructions to clean the wound and apply an antibiotic cream and a bandage twice a day for a week.

This would be a good time to tell you that, when they were handing out the contortionist genes, I went to the line marked "Tin Man" by mistake.

It's hard enough for me to put a bandage anywhere on my back. Trying to get it on a specific spot while using a mirror is like trying to find Jupiter with a cheap telescope.

I love my son John, but all I care about him at times like this is that he represents an additional pair of hands, unless I can get the emphysemic old lady next door to disconnect from her oxygen tank long enough to play nurse twice a day.

The problem is, John lives with me on alternate weeks, none of which ever falls on the week of my dermatology appointment. I think my wife had that written into the fine print of the divorce settlement.

As for that dry ice treatment ... About two days later, all those "pss" sounds the little canister made translate into an equal number of red blotches on my face. These then form little scabs. Again, per my divorce agreement, they are timed to appear just before a job interview, or any time a female I'm attracted to is in estrus.

I can't tell you how overjoyed I am to relive this experience four or five times a year.

Meanwhile, my kidney keeps on humming.

So does my dermatologist.

POETRY II

This is Part 2 of the author's epic foray into the world of competitive poetry. I call it

Poetry: The Sequel

It occurred to me after the last column that some of you may have thought the whole thing was a put-on, that there is no such poem as *I Am A Dad With Adult A.D.D.* Actually, the poem is real, but before I share it with you, let me say a few words about adult attention-deficit disorder.

Like poetry, adult attention-deficit disorder is a real problem for many of us. It doesn't get the attention it deserves – especially from those who have it.

Now back to the original topic.

As I sit here holding in my hand the Editor's Choice Award presented to John Shields for Outstanding Achievement in Poetry, I am awed to have come so far so fast. If I had any doubts about my poetic ability – and, friends, we poets have our moments of self-doubt like everyone else – this latest mailing from Poetry.com puts them to rest.

At the top of the page, above the tear-off certificate, is a handwritten note from one of the select judges to Howard Ely, managing editor of the International Library of Poetry. "Howard," it reads, "John's verse is wonderfully expressive – I suggest you use it for the 'Sound of Poetry.'" It is signed, simply, "CS." Like the great C.S. Eliot.

So, not only will I have my own page in *Eternal Portraits*, and not only have I been presented the detachable Editor's Choice Award, but I'm to have my artistry recorded professionally and featured in a "highly acclaimed and internationally distributed three-album collection," in which "Captivating Baroque music forms the background to the spoken words."

Did Keats ever have it this good?

This exposure to the upper echelons of the poetry world has taught me much. For example, I learned that many of my fellow poets have asked if the

International Library of Poetry can "make available a commemorative plaque to present their poetry in formal fashion."

And here I thought *I* was the only one with that idea.

You may not believe this, but it turns out they can actually do that. My poem can be "beautifully typeset on archive-quality vellum with choice of borders, then mounted on a walnut-finish plaque under lucite."

You have to think that someone like Walt Whitman would've appreciated having each of his poems mounted this way. Ah, the onomatopoeic sound of plaques clacking as we page through *Leaves of Grass*.

So much acclaim has come my way in such a short time that a skeptic couldn't be faulted for suggesting that someone is trying to stroke my ego to get me to buy something.

Fortunately, I know better. If they really wanted me to buy something, they would keep at it, wouldn't they, instead of telling me "This is your last opportunity to do so."

So, without further A.D.D.-do, and with the captivating strains of Vivaldi in the background, I present (in iambic pentameter) *I Am a Dad with Adult A.D.D.*:

> I am a dad with Adult A.D.D.
> As such there's much I oft initiate
> My desk and floor now hold some fifty-three
> Projects the start of which just couldn't wait.
> The papers thereon never find their rest
> Their sundry subjects saying, "We're still here."
> To find completion, that's my biggest test
> And something that I'll never do, I fear.
> So, rather than address the tasks at hand
> What does my fickle mind decide to do?
> It does something that wasn't even planned
> And spends its time on verse to send to you.

The Muse is with me. I think I can bring
That thousand-dollar prize home here to me!
I'll be right back, just have to do one thing ...
I am a dad with Adult A.D.D.

PERSPECTIVE

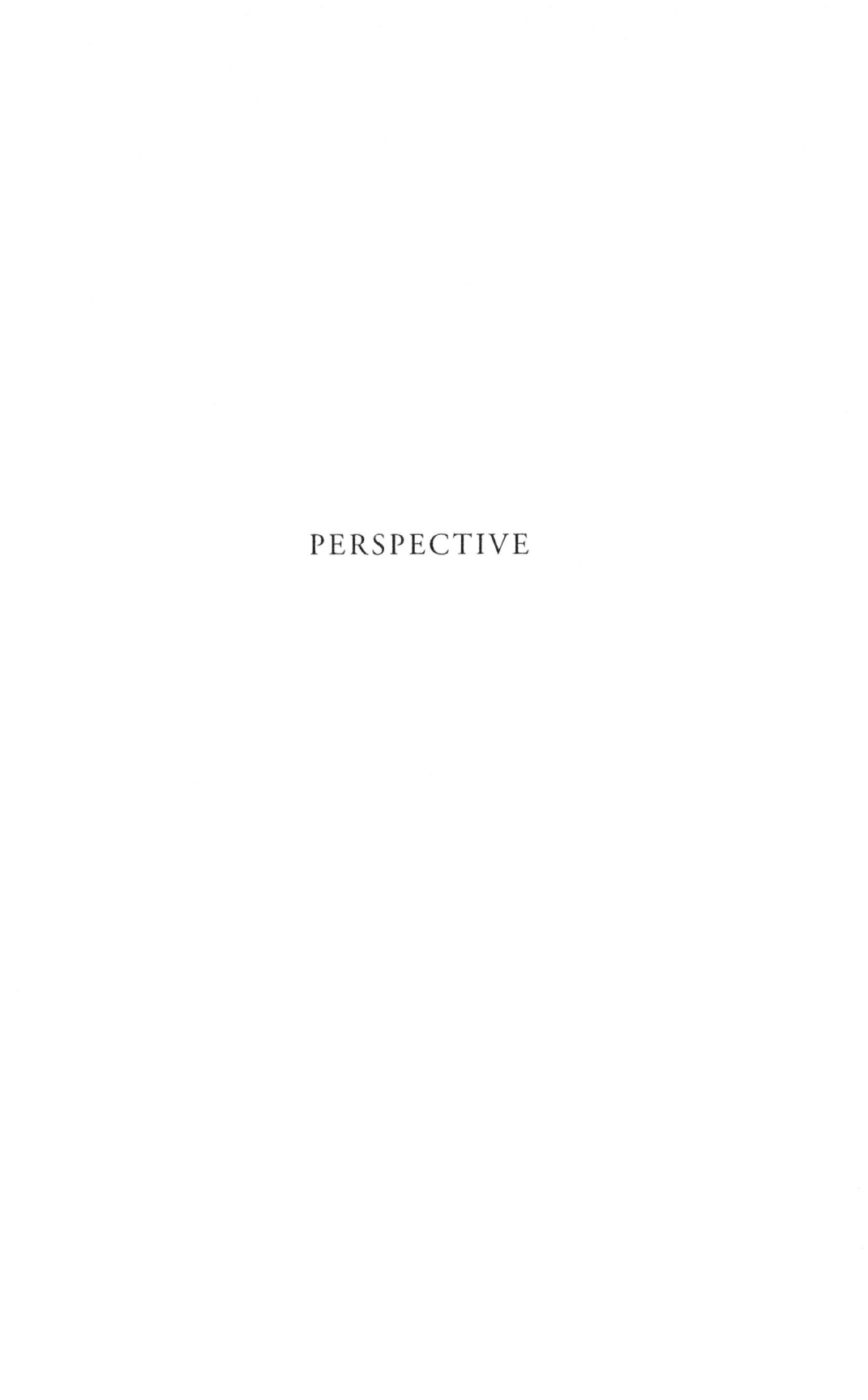

Let's get philosophical about work avoidance.

Ruminating on Sloth

Ever since reading John Osborne's play *Luther*, about the influential theologian and reformer Martin Luther, I've been hard at work ruminating on sloth.

And before you protest that ruminating is not exactly what you'd call work, let me say that I anticipated that response and have prepared the following airtight defense, as taught me by the Jesuits:

The dictionary defines "work" as "activity involving mental or physical effort done in order to achieve a purpose or result." It defines "ruminating" as "thinking deeply about something." Since "thinking" is defined as "using one's mind actively to form connected ideas," and "using one's mind actively" is synonymous with "mental effort," then it must follow that rumination is work.

Let's get that established so no one confuses it with daydreaming.

Sloth, too, is a problematic word. Many do not know how to pronounce it, nor do they know what it means. Does it rhyme with "both" or with "broth?" Or both? Maybe it rhymes with "Goth." And isn't it a creature, or am I confusing it with a slug? Answer: No, I'm not. It's also the name for a slow-moving, tropical mammal that hangs upside down from tree branches. Its slow-moving nature is probably what causes many of you – but not me – to confuse it with a slug.

See? Sloth gets your mind working, which makes it a paradox: a word meaning "laziness" that causes you to work.

Whew, my brain needs a break. All this ruminating wears you out. No wonder cows look so sluggish all the time. Being a ruminant is hard work.

But back to sloth. In the Christian tradition, it's one of the seven deadly sins, known by their formal title, The Seven Deadly Sins. The others are pride, covetousness, lust, anger, gluttony, and rumination. This is relevant information as we work our way back to *Luther*. (I should point out here that Osborne's *Luther* is not to be confused with the more obscure *Luthier*. You'll recall that that play was about a rebellious maker of stringed instruments. His condemnation of the sale of indulgences – though he made an exception for Dove Bars and Hostess Twinkies – and his belief in the tonal superiority of the fretless bass created a schism in the music industry.)

But back to sloth and Luther. This, from the opening scene of Osborne's play ... Act One, Scene One. *The sun has not yet risen, but the monks are up.* (Isn't that always the case with monks?) *They are confessing their sins to the abbot. One monk berates himself for his sin of sloth*:

"Twice in my sloth I have omitted to shave, and even excused myself, pretending to believe my skin fairer than that of my Brothers, and my beard lighter and my burden also."

Prior to reading that, I'd had a very different conception of what sloth was. My idea of sloth was lying on the sofa watching Sport Center for the twelfth time, the domestic landscape strewn with empty pizza boxes and crusted salsa.

"If a missed shave now and then is sloth," I thought, "we are all doomed to hell." Because if that's sloth, what would you call throwing your socks and undershirts in the hamper inside out for someone else to reverse? Or weed-whacking every fourth grass cutting? Or your teenager's bedroom?

Ubersloth?

But, kidding aside, what impressed me about the monk's admission was the lofty standard he had set for himself. He recognized the insidious temptation to not only kick back but to rationalize it.

Who among us, when confronted with the choice of living the moment diligently or living it lethargically, hasn't chosen the latter?

The seeds of full-blown sloth are contained in the little choices we make each day – leaving the cap off the toothpaste; returning food items to no further than the front of the refrigerator shelf (wait, maybe that's prudence); anything pertaining to the remote ...

Now whether the pace of sixteenth-century monastic life can compare to the frenetic pace of the 21st century is a matter for historians with stopwatches. Perhaps a monk's sloth is modernity's sanity. But hidden somewhere in that mortified monk's day-old stubble is a lesson in right living worth ruminating about.

In the absence of truly knowing others, why do we feel we can judge them, often unfairly and by such shallow criteria?

Reunion, Reconsideration

It's high school reunion time again for this great alumnus ... sorry, *grayed* alumnus. I've attended probably half of these quinquennial events (from the Latin meaning "every five years," as *quinque* of my fellow St. Joe's Prep classmates could tell you). The passage of years brings perspective and a fair measure of wisdom, gifts I wouldn't trade for any of the baser qualities associated with the salad days.

Raging libido, maybe.

I told one of the event's organizers that one classmate I hope to see this time – and it would be the first time since we graduated – is Joe Kline.

"Boringly studious" would be one way of describing Joe Kline. The yearbook lists Sodality, Community Action Program, Band, Dramatics, Honor Society and Student Film Festival as his extracurricular activities.

(Aside: I'd love to explain to non-Catholics out there what "Sodality" means, but I've never known what it means myself. It's one of those church things that you go to when they put you into it. I think it means "the quality of being sodal," if that's any help.)

From the perspective of a fellow 17-year-old at the time, Kline's pursuits spelled N-E-R-D to me. (Me, who listed four years in the Boosters as his sole extracurricular activity.) Looking at them through adult eyes, however, I see a sensitive young "man for others," with creativity, self-discipline, and a calling or two.

Born and raised in similar, blue-collar, manufacturing neighborhoods, Joe and I were among the small number of students who studied Greek at the Prep, so we shared the same homeroom for three years. Except for the humiliating boxing sessions we all had to endure in gym class, the only time

I saw him in action outside the classroom was when he played the organ at *liturgies*. (See *sodality* above.)

Joe went on to study music, first at the Curtis Institute and then at the Juilliard School in New York. During his final year at Juilliard, he performed Bach's complete organ works in 14 recitals at several Manhattan venues. The *Christian Science Monitor* remarked on the Bach series in an editorial, and the *New York Times* ran a feature article on the then-21-year-old. He reprised his performance the following year in Philadelphia and was a featured soloist at the Academy of Music.

I obtained this and the following information about Joe from his website when I decided to contact him myself about the reunion. It's the website for Mepkin Abbey, a Trappist monastery in South Carolina. The biographical information is from Joe's obituary.

Joe Kline, or Father Francis, as he was known, died of cancer there on August 27, 2006. He'd been Mepkin's abbot since 1990.

Joe became a Trappist monk not long after his prodigious Bach recitals. As Abbott Francis, he gave retreats, lectured, and published articles on monasticism and spirituality. He authored the book, *Lovers of the Place: Monasticism Loose in the Church*, and he was finishing a second book in the months before his death.

He also worked with the environmental community to preserve open space. Under his leadership, two weeks before he died, 3,100 acres owned by the monastery were protected in perpetuity from commercial development.

During his tenure as abbot, Mepkin built a new church, a library and conference center, and a senior wing for aging monks. It also renovated the monks' kitchen and refectory, guests' refectory, and administration building.

I should be so nerdish.

As an only child comfortable being alone but needing the company of friends, I've long been fascinated by the monastic lifestyle, with its atmosphere of prayerful solitude within a community structure. Somewhere along the way, I determined that the most challenging, most courageous, most fulfilling way for me to live was as a secular monk. In the world *and* of it, full tilt in the ways that count, but otherwise sparingly, selectively.

I'd known of Joe's monastic life from a news article I'd read on his election as abbott. Then, while channel-surfing one evening, I found a PBS documentary called "Trappist," and there he was, playing the organ at a monastic liturgy and, later, speaking on camera.

I should visit him, I thought.

How many times did I state my intention to do that, only to see my life – as parent, husband, coach, chronic patient – lay first claim?

Now it's too late.

Two Joe Kline quotes will stay with me, however. The first is one he spoke often to his fellow monks near the end of his life: "How can I be worthy of such graces, of such a contemplative experience?"

The other he wrote in my senior yearbook before we parted for separate paths, each of us, in his own way, choosing "the road less traveled":

> *Don't goof off, John*
> *Joe Kline III*

Through four years of high school, Joe and I exchanged maybe 200 words, and half of those were in Greek and the other half were variations of "Hi, Joe" and "Hi, John." But in the clear mirror of hindsight, I recognize the above four he wrote as the most insightful, and least heeded, of all the sentiments penned me by classmates in that book of memories.

In a way that Joe, above all, understood, I have had my reunion with him this week after all. As he's shown, our attendance at the next is not guaranteed.

I'd better get cracking.

The annual Perseid and Leonid meteor showers are a celestial gift to us earthbound wonderers. Too bad we can't see them.

Notes From a Backyard Stargazer

A moonless night, the occasional soft breeze brushing the neck, conveying what perfect weather feels like. Almost mid-August and the crickets are active, ranging from an abrasive, call-and-response chirp to the more musical sound we recognize when we hear one in some corner of the garage.

It's just after midnight on the 13th, and that, along with the new moon, makes it the best time for viewing this year's Perseid meteor shower. The "meteors" are actually debris from the comet Swift-Tuttle, but they've been meteors to me ever since I first saw them in a coal-black Maine sky three decades ago.

I'm square in a chair in the middle of my back yard, a ready spectator.

I phoned my son John at his mom's house about an hour ago with the heads up, which is a minimum requirement for spotting anything in the night sky.

John loves all things cosmic. When he and his brother and sister were little, I'd haul the third-rate telescope I'd bought out to the backyard and try whipping them into a frenzy over astronomical events – we had a run on comets back then – even when the events turned out to be duds.

I considered it something a dad ought to do. There's more to life than ball sports.

Nick and Chloe tolerated my eccentricity, unaware that I was infusing them with the poetic soul, but, in John, my own love affair with the heavens took root.

I'm still waiting for my eyes to adapt to the dark, but that's not the only obstacle blocking my vision of the Perseids. My next-door neighbors' oak tree obliterates a wide swath of the eastern sky, in the direction I'm supposed to be looking. Other nearby mature trees consume their own chunk of the firmament, leaving the open vault directly overhead as my only unobstructed view.

Then there's the light from my neighbors' house. Kevin and Pam lost a child some years ago, and in his memory they keep a porch light and window candles on through the night, year round. Am I to complain over such an infusion of brightness and love? Besides, a single house's light isn't what's robbing us of the stars.

Gazing up from my lawn chair, I'm beginning to make out stars that weren't visible a scant ten minutes ago. There are so few to be seen in the sky anymore. Three nights from now I'll be out west with my three children. We'll spend time in national parks. I'm hoping the night sky there will be spectacular for them. Can we give our kids a better gift than firsthand knowledge of a sky teeming with stars?

My neighbors' porch light illuminates the tips of leaves on a nearby maple, fooling the eye into momentarily thinking it's seen something meteor-like. I phone John for an update. Our respective skies are too bright. He's seen nary a Perseid so far and is ready for bed. I've seen nothing either, but I opt to wait. There's poetry in the air, on schedule or not. I should not be too impatient to leave it.

Minutes pass, and then a single piece of comet debris flashes directly overhead, again further left, and still a third time to the left of that.

I wait for more, but that's all I see of the Perseids. A galactic ellipsis. The Creator's unfinished thought ...

Hadrons? Hardons? What's the difference if we're not gonna be here much longer?

When Black Holes Have Earth for Lunch

On November 9, 1965, at 5:28 pm, a housewife in Queens plugged her coffee percolator into a wall outlet and a split second later, all of New York City went dark. It was the Great Blackout of 1965, and the housewife thought she had caused it

Whether true or apocryphal, it's a great story, and it popped into my head this morning when I read that tomorrow is the day the Large Hadron Collider gets turned on.

The Large Hadron Collider is both a big machine and a 17-mile circular tunnel 300 feet underground, beneath France and Switzerland. It took 9 billion dollars, 7000 scientists, and 20 years to build, but, finally, it's ready for its mission: to recreate the conditions of the early universe, just a trillionth of a second after the Big Bang.

It's a project so long in the making, in fact, that some of the older scientists who were around at its inception can't recall now whether "large" refers to the size of the hadrons or the size of the collider.

I hope you're not expecting me to know the answer.

Scientists would like everyone to think that "hadron" has some subatomic definition, because that makes it easier for them to finagle grant money. And by the way, if you're grant writing for your own particle-physics experiment, always remember to add "-on" to the end of your particle's name. That's because everything inside an atom ends in "-on": electron, proton, neutron, baryon, carry-on. ...

Except for quarks.

A little-known fact about the Large Hadron Collider is that, because of its proximity to the Tour de France, its designers have been using pharmacologically disqualified Tour cyclists to "road test" the interior of the particle accelerator.

"Since the speed of the particle beams will reach 99.99 percent of the speed of light," said project coordinator N.R. Jizer, "we felt that cyclists who'd taken performance-enhancing drugs would be best equipped to attain comparable speeds as we fine tune the Collider for the big day."

And that big day is tomorrow, when some obscure, Stephen Hawking-wannabe astrophysicist is going to do, essentially, what that Queens housewife did in her kitchen forty-some years ago: plug in an appliance.

Only this appliance is the circumference of Philadelphia.

And that has some people worried. They're the people who believe a "hadron" is not a subatomic particle but an acronym for **Has A Disastrous Repercussion ... Oh, No!**

They're afraid, you see, that the Collider may create black holes that will devour the earth.

(And our friend in Queens thought *she* had a great cause-and-effect story.)

The creators of the Large Hadron Collider say that such fears are groundless. (Maybe not the best word when talking about electro-magnetism.) One of them, Professor Brian Cox of Manchester University, has even gone so far as to say, "Anyone who thinks the LHC will destroy the world is a t---t." (In England, calling someone a "t---t" is the nastiest form of put down. Worse than being called a "t---t," even.)

And Lord Rees of the Royal Society assures us that the amount of energy released by the colliding large hardons will be "comparable to that of two colliding mosquitoes," which doesn't say much for hardons. But to Lord Rees I say, "What if you're wrong? What if the 'mc' in Einstein's $E=mc^2$ stands for 'mosquito collision' and not 1,100?"

He hasn't gotten back to me on that one.

Sure, maybe the Large Hadron Collider *will* give us answers about the Higgs boson, and, yes, the Tevatron out there at the Fermi Lab just can't cut it anymore. But when all those newly created black holes start devouring Earth the second after that astrophysicist plugs in the Collider tomorrow, I plan to pile on the guilt real thick and tell him (if there's time) that yes, pal, it was you who caused it.

A missed room reservation, a relative beheaded, and the wine runs out at a wedding. All that's missing is a betrayal ... wait, no it's not.

The Serious World of The New Testament

Through the years I've been characterized by some as too serious. "Lighten up," they've advised, and I've taken that advice very seriously.

If, in fact, I *am* too serious, I think I know the reason why, and it has nothing to do with my family upbringing. My family was a fun-loving bunch. Well, except for my dad, whose moroseness could make a sinkhole look like a dental cavity.

I'm going to get in trouble here, but the editor told me that politics was the only off-limit topic for this column. So here goes. The real source of my gravity, my ponderousness, is the Roman Catholic religion in which I was so efficiently schooled as a child.

Forget the Old Testament for a minute, not that it's exactly a bastion of levity, and page through the New Testament Gospels. You'll have about as much luck finding a smile or a joke as Diogenes had looking for an honest man. From the first word in Matthew ("A") to the last in John ("them"), the "good news" of the Gospels makes them the KYW of their day: "All seriousness all the time."

Think about it. For starters, although they had to have known it was going to be a busy week in Bethlehem, Joseph and Mary failed to reserve a hotel room and were stuck with what was left.

Soon after the Big Event (joyful, yes; funny, I don't think so), they're forced to flee to Egypt because Herod's paranoid about a day-old rival to his throne.

When he's eight days old, Jesus is circumcised. Ouch. Then his mother is told by an old man she's never met before, Simeon, that she'll be pierced with a sword.

After this initial flurry of uprootedness and pain both physical and psychological, and a later episode where Jesus's parents discover He's missing, we fast-forward to the years before Jesus's crucifixion. His cousin John is beheaded. Demons abound. Every second person He meets is either blind or a leper. The dead need raising. The living are either poor, lowly or sorrowing – or all three. And at a wedding feast in Cana, the wine runs out. Jesus does remedy the situation there, but only after everyone's pissed about the empty barrels.

You'd think that somewhere in the Parables, Jesus would let loose a little Seinfeldian cynicism that would give us all a chuckle. Instead, they're all about vindictive masters, scheming servants, and corrupt judges.

Throughout, Jesus, who is every Christian's ultimate role model, is never described as "jovial" or "merry." Nothing He says or does ever seems said or done "in jest." On the contrary, even He Himself seems set upon by the strain of all this seriousness. He zaps a fig tree because it was fruitless when He was hungry. Inside the Temple, He goes ballistic on the money changers.

Then the *really* serious stuff begins. Peter whacks a guy's ear off. Judas betrays Jesus then hangs himself. For heaven's sake, for *our* sakes, couldn't we use a little George Carlin about now?

Scourging, bureaucratic failure to accept responsibility, crucifixion, death and burial. Even the Resurrection accounts are colored by apprehension and uncertainty.

Subliminally, what was all this saying to impressionable youngsters like me? Then, layer on it such man-made constructs as Limbo and Purgatory and you have the makings of one serious individual.

Me.

And no matter how much I'd like to lighten up, no matter how whimsical or recklessly indulgent I'd care to be, I'm the product of a 2000-year-old institution that's had plenty of practice in staying on-message.

World religions, I'll concede, are powerful and compelling philosophies that ought not undergo too many permutations. Deservedly so. But is it asking too much to see Jesus or Mohammed slip on a banana peel every once in awhile?

DEUCE

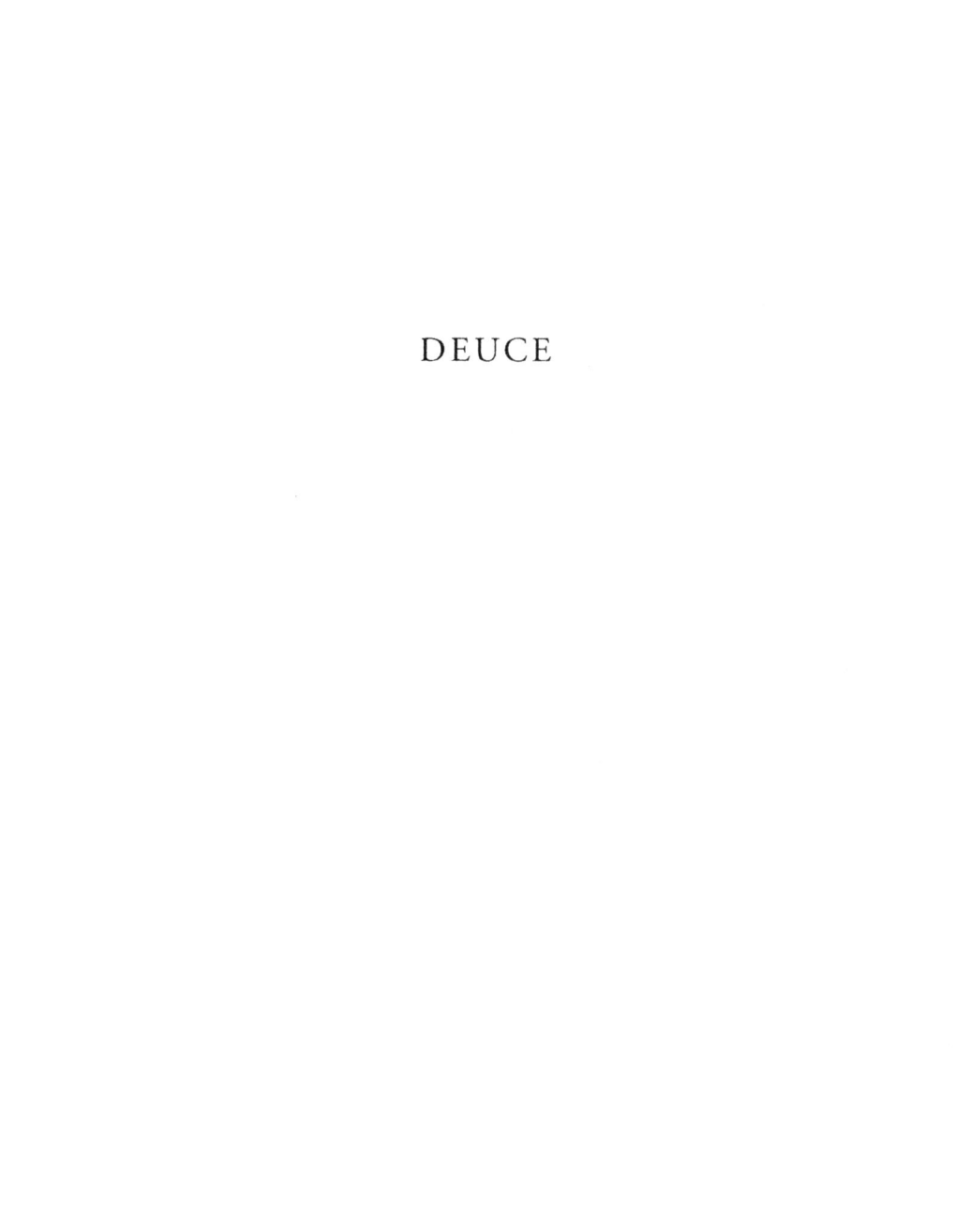

You know your life's humdrum when you get into a pissing match with your cat. Well, not a literal pissing match.

"Not the Pictures, John!"

Sunday night, my house. Not the most compelling part of town. I'd just finished vacuuming the basement and, yes, the basement steps. You may recall vacuuming the basement steps as among the Least Essential Household Tasks.

I can sense you questioning, "What's he doing vacuuming the basement on a Sunday night?" The more perceptive among you are even adding, "Let alone the steps."

I'm just going to ignore it.

Having vacuumed my way up the steps after doing the basement, I was sitting in the kitchen, rewinding the power cord. My cat, Deuce, was on the kitchen table, keeping me company. Yes, that's right, his name is slang for the voided waste material some people call "number two." Look, I did not name the cat. My kids named the cat. I merely signed off on it, thinking it more along the lines of a riverboat gambler.

Like all cats, Deuce is curious, and he was fixated on this act of wrapping the cord onto the vacuum cleaner. After all, what's a power cord to a cat except a longer, thicker version of string?

I noticed his fascination, so I decided to tease him and break the silence of a humdrum, monastic day. "See this?" I said, making a cord wrapping gesture. "This is something I can do that you can't."

In hindsight, I probably should have held my tongue, but I wasn't sure I could one-up him doing that.

"Maybe," he replied, "but here's something I can do that *you* can't."

With that, he leaped headfirst off the table.

I've never leaped headfirst off any table, though I did convey my second thoughts about neck surgery once by attempting to *roll* off the one in the operating room.

"You got me there," I said.

I thought a minute, and popped open the vacuum cleaner cover to check the bag. "Can *you* check the bag?" I asked him, knowing I was safe in asking that. "You can't even open the cover."

"No, but can you do this?" He raised his hind leg perpendicular to the floor and licked his butt clean.

Just to show him that I could be a clean freak too, I replaced the old bag with a new one.

He responded by coughing up a fur ball. "A little something for your new bag."

He looked around knowingly, slightly bobbing his head as he did so, as if acknowledging the approval of fellow cats.

That gave me an idea. I applauded. "Let's see *you* applaud, Deuce."

He could grasp with his two front paws, but he was incapable of putting them together repetitively to acknowledge a sentiment agreed with or a job well done. And he knew it. "Damn!" he muttered under his breath.

I seized on this weakness and challenged him to a game of hot hands. It was so one-sided that in the middle of the game he turned and walked away, feigning indifference.

Game. Set. Match. Or so I thought.

I was putting the vacuum away when Deuce called out from his spot on the sofa. "Yo! Mister Dexterity. Let's see how good you are without your hands." Then he arched his head back over his shoulder and cleaned the middle of his back with his tongue.

"Can I use a loofah?" I asked.

"Only if you put it in your mouth."

He had me on that one.

Now *he* was the one on the offensive. "C'mon outside," he said. I followed him, winning a round in passing when he couldn't open the sliding door for himself. "Try this," he gloated, as he leaped onto the top of a chain-link fence and walked along it tightrope-style.

Then, almost as if he were rubbing it in, he jumped from the fence, retrieved the dead bird he'd killed earlier in the day and dropped it at my feet. "Not a gift, 'Master.' A demonstration," he smirked.

"Demonstration?" I cried. "Demonstration?" I thrust my arm toward him and grabbed his tail – he'd made a point of showing me all that he could do with that, too – and was about to commence the Fling of Death when I heard him plead, "John. John. It's me, Deuce. Your pal."

And we *are* pals. I regained control of my emotions (something I don't believe cats can do, by the way) and gave him a good, long petting. He purred and purred (which I don't believe humans can do) and asked me to bring him back into the house.

Once inside, I put him down. (No, not *that* "put him down.") He set right to clawing away at the carpet, a form of one-upsmanship that I know just how to handle: I tie him to a scratching post and make him look at pictures of declawed felines.

He gets the point.

Creatures that I've shared a home with, human or otherwise, don't get fat. They just don't. That includes dogs, hamsters, goldfish, crickets and lizards. So what's up with my cat … besides his weight, that is?

Ab Crunches for Tabby?

My cat is fat. Rotund. Obese. (Could this be a poem?) He's now a feline of such girth that, Lord, I hardly know him. (ta-da)

Deuce – that's my cat – wasn't always fat. He was just big, the way some people are big. "Big-boned" is the expression, right?

So let's concede that my cat is big-boned. At his last visit to the vet, though, he weighed in at 16 pounds, 6 ounces.

"Holy catfood! What did he weigh last time?" I asked.

"When he was here eight months ago he was fourteen four."

I quick ran the arithmetic. A jump of two pounds two ounces in two-thirds of a year.

Then I ran the algebra. The old "percent change" calculation. A 16 percent increase. That'd be like me going from 170 to 197. Over two decades of marriage, maybe, but in eight months? Even Seventh Day Adventists would be calling for my blood work.

"How could that be?" I wondered aloud. He's an indoor-outdoor cat, which in my book means he's getting daily exercise. Could the occasional meal of field mouse or newly un-nested bird account for the size of the creature here before us, a creature that tests the limits of my floor joists with every step he takes? No way.

The vet showed me a chart. I felt like the character in *Clockwork Orange* who was forced to look at disturbing images. "Look at these silhouettes of cats," she said, "then pick out the one that most looks like Deuce."

If I were honest with myself, I would've selected the stability ball with whiskers at the far end of the scale, but I couldn't face the shame of recognition, so I chose the one just before it – the beach ball. The difference between the two was negligible: each had a body wildly disproportionate to its head size and a pronounced, dangling "fat pad" on its underbelly.

"Oh, so that's what that is," I marveled. I'd always assumed that soft, pouchy area on Deuce's belly was a side effect of neutering. You know, lost muscle tone. That sort of thing.

Since her goal in this exercise was to get me to acknowledge Deuce's fatness, the vet diplomatically concurred with my choice of the beach ball – I'm sure she sees this behavior all the time – and then she introduced me to a cat-food concept heretofore alien to me: calories.

Flashing some brand literature, she gave me a couple low-cal alternatives. I settled on Science Diet Light at 312 calories per cup, reasoning that Stephen Hawking is a scientist and he doesn't seem to have a fat pad.

That day, I embarked on the alliterative "Deuce's Diet" and fed him the recommended daily six ounces. Five diligent weeks later, I took him back to the vet for a second weigh-in.

He had lost three ounces. Three @#$&! *ounces*.

"Are you playing with him?" the vet asked me.

"I tease him about his fat pad, if that's what you mean."

"No. I mean string, feathers, cat toys. Make him chase you through the house."

I draw the line at string. Oh, occasionally, from my desk chair, I'll dangle my shoelace if it happens to be on my foot. If the cat happens to be passing by, he may take a swipe at it. So, yes, Doctor animal doctor, I do play with my cat.

I could defend my integrity all I wanted, but Deuce's weight gain and seeming inability to lose it remained perplexing. That's when my newly heightened awareness of cat calories came in handy.

For the past few years I've varied up Deuce's regular cat food every couple of weeks by substituting a bag of treats for that day's portion. At three ounces, it's half the weight of his usual food. This time, and for the first time, I read the label. Who'd expect that something half the weight would contain *13 times the mass* and not be called plutonium? Neither would I, but there it was: 4,000 calories.

The equivalent of two weeks' meals in a day. Every two weeks.

So the puzzle's been solved, and we've since signed on to a less sedentary lifestyle. Deuce is appreciative of his new regimen, I think. I found a feathery boa at the pet store that has him pouncing like he was a kitten again. That and a length of silver Christmas ribbon are his speed bag and stationary bike. He gets his cardio chasing me from the kitchen sink to the kitchen table. (Hey, I'm not the one with the weight problem.)

As for those treats, maybe Stephen Hawking should try them. They come in fish flavors as well as meat, and he can afford to put on a pound or two.

FINDINGS II

As told by Dave Barry at a columnists' conference ... A writer and an editor are stuck in the desert when they come upon an oasis. They crawl to the water, whereupon the editor proceeds to piss into it. The writer is appalled. "What are you doing?!" The editor replies, "Making it better."

How Komodo Dragons Affect the Fishing Industry

Correction:

Last week's "Ab Crunches for Tabby?" column contained what can rightly be termed a gross exaggeration. In changing my cat's weight to 144 pounds where I'd had him at "fourteen four," the paper's acting editor, Nancy Prufreid, led you to believe that my cat Deuce had dropped 130 pounds.

Domestic cats do not attain weights of 144 pounds. The heftiest top out around 24, though my cousin Bobby once got his Siamese, Sumo, pushing 60 on a diet of mortadella and cannolis. During drought season, Serengeti lions, at 700 pounds, may experience a slim-down of the magnitude attributed to Deuce. (Wildlife biologists and English majors refer to it as getting "svelte on the veldt.") But those leonine love handles invariably return. That's what wildebeests are for.

Deuce not being a Serengeti lion, I apologize for any confusion that you may have experienced. A 130-pound weight loss is serious tonnage, even for humans. Don't try this at home on your own cat or you'll create anti-matter.

Sincerely,
The author

Continuing in the wildlife vein, it's time once again to see what *Harper's* "Findings" page has to tell us about the natural – and unnatural – world we live in. (These are not made up.)

I've put them in the form of a matching test. Pair the finding with the commentary (mine) that accompanies it. Best, I think, to first read the Findings in their entirety and then tackle the Comments one at a time. The answers are at the bottom, right side up ... because I don't know how to turn them upside down.

Great research knows no geographical, or even planetary, boundaries. Nine countries and a galaxy are represented.

FINDINGS

    A. Entomologists tricked Argentine ants into disposing of live pupae by dousing the living antlings with the smell of the dead.
    B. An English hedgehog suffering from spinelessness was taken to Tiggywinkles Wildlife Hospital in Buckinghamshire.
    C. The center of the Milky Way tastes like raspberries and smells like rum.
    D. Kentucky is the saddest state.
    E. A professor of clothing at Japan's Women's University invented stink-free underwear for astronauts.
    F. Italian scientists studying the gas that makes rotten eggs and flatulence stink announced that the substance may work as an impotence drug after they injected it into the excised penises of sex-change patients.
    G. In Hawaii, a woman found a $5 bill inside a coconut.
    H. An Indonesian fisherman was killed by Komodo dragons when he attempted to collect sugar apples from a dragon-infested forest.
    I. A chimpanzee in Sweden was found to be stockpiling weapons to use against humans.
    J. Twitter dulls compassion for human suffering.
    K. Surgeons in Russia removed a fir sapling from a man's lungs.
    L. Swarms of immortal jellyfish were spreading through the world's oceans.
    M. In western Iran, the growing popularity of *taqaandan*, a pastime in which the top half of the erect penis is wrenched sharply to one side and "popped," and which has led to an epidemic of penile fractures, was becoming a public-health concern.

N. Cows with names produce 3.4 percent more milk than nameless cows.

COMMENTARY

1. All this time I thought abject despondency was.
2. Hey, tree svinger! Ja, sticks and stönes may ban break our bönes, but ...
3. Let them eat tweets.
4. Starring Vincent Price as Arturo, the antomologist, in "The Premature Burial."
5. Now that's a (hono) lulu!
6. The obvious question: Why just astronauts?
7. He was admitted to the Cowardly Lion ward.
8. Serves him right. What's a fisherman doing in a forest anyway?
9. Wrapped in a creamy, dark-matter chocolate.
10. And we consider this country a threat?
11. Led by the world-renowned Lois Pasture.
12. Adding to the lore that Italian men – and women? – make the best lovers.
13. Newspaper headline: *A Tree Grows in Roosk's Lung*
14. Our only defense? The Jersey Shore.

ANSWERS: A-4, B-7, C-9, D-1, E-6, F-12, G-5, H-8, I-2, J-3, K-13, L-14, M-10, N-11

DIY

One wood planer to the first reader who can identify what's getting planed.

If Fencing Referred Only to Swords

You'd think by now that, with all our technological acumen, we would've invented a Permanently Straight Fence Gate

As we all know, Mother Nature has traditionally relied on a few simple stratagems for tormenting humans: hurricanes, tornados, and raising and lowering our fence posts. Of course, she doesn't directly raise and lower our fence posts, in the same way that the Fed doesn't directly raise or lower our interest rates. No, she creates freeze-and-thaw cycles to do the job.

Fence gates may look like simple operations, but they're actually a Euclidean nightmare of angles and clearances. Do something over here to one part and another part over there starts misbehaving.

One day you come home from work, pulling the gate closed behind you, when you notice that the latch that used to slide right into the little hole now hits just beneath the hole. To the naked eye, nothing has changed, but somewhere, Mother Nature is splitting a gut

You have two options: Option A) raise the gate, or Option B) lower the hole.

My own gate has been out of line so long it won the Animal House Lifetime Achievement Award. Last weekend, I finally got around to fixing it.

There are two cardinal rules I adhere to when tackling home repairs:

Rule 1: The farther the job from my tools, the fewer tools I will bring to the job. I call this the "Inverse Tool Law."

And Rule 2: Never leave well enough alone.

From my two gate options (not to be confused with my two cardinal rules) I chose Option A: raising the gate – or at least the latch plate on the gate.

I figured all I needed was my socket wrench, to loosen a couple of bolts. But then I saw I needed a hammer to knock one of them out of its hole in the gate, so it was *back into the house* for a hammer.

After driving the bolt out, I decided I should lubricate it so its nut would thread back on more easily. I went *back into the house* for some WD40.

That detour opened the gate (heh heh) for Rule 2: Never leave well enough alone.

I decided to try raising the gate on its hinge side.

To do that, I needed a combination wrench, which I didn't have (see Rule 1), so I went *back into the house* for it.

I unloosened the hinge with the combination wrench, and then tried tightening down the hinge post by hand. I couldn't budge it, so I went *back into the house* for a pair of pliers.

They didn't help.

Then I thought maybe I could raise the gate by slipping a washer or two onto the post before putting the hinge back on.

Here we see the two rules working as a team.

Naturally, I didn't bring washers out to the fence initially because what do washers have to do with fences? and vice versa, so I had to go *back into the house* for them

It was a clever idea, washers, but it meant having to re-drill the holes for the hinge, and even *I* wasn't crazy enough to do that.

Then I remembered my Swiss Army knife. I could use one or more of its nifty gadgets to ream out the hole and create a bigger opening for the latch to slide into.

(As you may have recognized, this represented a subtle shift to Option B: lowering the hole, something any rational person knew 300 words ago was what should've been done in the first place.)

The Swiss Army knife was *back in the house.*

I retrieved it, and, after five minutes of reaming, the latch slid in and out as easily as ... well, this is a family paper, so let's just say it slid in and out easily

It was the only tool I'd really needed

After I got the latch nicely lined up though, the gate was now brushing the fence post as it swung by (see "Euclidean nightmare"). Easy enough to fix – I just needed to shave a little off the gate with my wood planer – which was *back in the house.*

So, to recap: to realign my gate latch the EIGHTH OF AN INCH! it needed, I used a socket wrench set (metric and English), a hammer, WD40, a combination wrench, pliers, two washers, a Swiss Army knife, and a wood planer.

Not to feel too sorry for me, though. I burned 600 calories going back and forth, *and* I earned 1.5 Frequent Pliers miles.

For those who don't, it's helpful to know that "WC" stands for "water closet" and is an abbreviation for a toilet, or a room containing a toilet.

Call Me WC Shields

I was merely trying to remove the acrylic knob on my bathroom faucet so I could get at some long-standing soap scum, but the rusted screw holding the knob in place wasn't turning – and isn't there a Henry James do-it-yourself book on that very topic? Desperate, I pried the knob a bit too forcefully – the forcefully a construction worker might impart on a two-by-four with a crowbar. And, suuure ... *then* it came off easily enough.

It just wouldn't go back on, as things in shards are wont to do.

Having demolished the piece that controlled the water temperature, I knew I'd crossed a lavatorial Rubicon.

I would have to redo the entire room.

My bathroom, you see, was the kind of space depressives seek out when they want the proper ambience for sustained misery. Except for the toilet, every fixture and surface area was the color of either stool or diluted urine – the latter, at least, being a neutral. If you wanted to think of yourself as a worthless, voided substance, you came to the right rest room.

The walls were covered with circa-1968 linoleum that complemented the mudslide-brown bathtub. To brighten the mood – I'm guessing – the vanity bowl rim was scalloped – a popular look in the days when a scalloped-shaped sink screamed "quasi-affluence!" or "You're at the seashore!" but as out of place as a beached horseshoe crab here in land-locked Montgomery County, Pennsylvania

.

The toilet, an old 3.2-gallon Mansfield, was a performance giant for which "clog" meant a wooden-soled shoe and nothing more. But performance aside, no amount of whitening agent was going to erase the rust-induced rivulets of discoloration etched down the sides of the bowl. Along with the fake-parquet vinyl floor, they were another restatement of the room's UPS theme: Let brown do it.

Shattered knob and stripped screw in hand, I considered my options. Merely installing a shiny new faucet didn't strike me as providing sufficient, anti-depressive counterweight to the preponderance of … let's call them "earth tones." But I couldn't face the prospect of a full remodeling project, so for the next three months I used a pair of needle-nose pliers to make my temperature selections.

For guests, I left the pliers on the vanity, pointing like a directional arrow toward the knobless faucet, so that they could intuit their purpose as they hovered for a hand wash over the mollusk-themed basin.

What got me over the inertia hump was a friend offering his help with the demo. (That's shop talk for "demolition.") Together, we ripped out the linoleum, the sheetrock, the bathtub, the toilet, the vanity and the old insulation and chiseled away two layers of glued-down, probably-asbestos-laden sheet flooring. For most of the skilled jobs, I retained the services of professionals, who were glad for the work. I put the toilet and vanity in by myself. I also hung a new slab door on my own, something even waterboarding could not coerce me to do ever again. It's why they invented pre-hung doors – to quiet the keening of generations of do-it-yourselfers.

Neither of my knees bends anymore, but by doing as much of the labor as I could, I saved, as Elmer Fudd would say, "a wad of money." To replace all the plumbing and fixtures and upgrade the insulation, lighting, flooring and doors, the entire project – not counting my MRI – came in at just under $4,500 plus a case of beer for the plumber. In all, about half the average cost of remodeling an average bathroom.

With a pale blue paint scheme and white doors to match the new porcelain, what was once earth is now sky, while brown, which had in days gone by made the room so … shoe-colored, has seen its dominance dim, confined to the vanity base, where it plays but a supporting role.

As a homeowner, I try to use my head ...

Water on the Brain

My house's previous owners had a thing for filtered water, may they rot in Hades. Rather than installing a water purifier at the kitchen faucet like normal Americans, they favored the in-line, basement kind, the kind that tall guys like me keep trying to dislodge with our foreheads.

My model is the BT24 Whole House Prefiltration unit. The "BT" stands for "Blunt Trauma." Its filter has a six-month useful life, just long enough to ensure that I won't be able to remember how to replace it the next time.

The housing that holds the filter resembles one of those cylindrical tubes you see at a drive-in bank, the kind that travels invisibly to the window teller and back with your deposits, withdrawals, and this-is-a-robbery notes.

It's soldered directly into the water line, where the six inches of copper tubing that were hack-sawed out to accommodate it used to be.

I don't have to tell you: Homeowners instinctively abhor a six-inch break in their water lines.

The problem with filters of this design is that you're stuck with the arrangement, unless you want to part with $150 or so to have the plumber undo it. I figure for that much money, at two filters a year, I can keep the water in my house sediment-free for the next thirty years. By that time, mankind will have run out of water or drowned in too much of it, and filtration will be a moot point.

The disturbingly hard plastic housing hangs vertically from the water line a distance of about a foot. My head rises up from my shoulders about the same distance. So when the two meet unexpectedly – and they do – the impact (see "Blunt Trauma") forces an expletive from my mouth.

After a few of these blows, I notice I'm beginning to slur my expletives. I ask my neurologist what my prognosis is. "Not good if you keep the filter," he tells me.

I begin thinking that sediment directly into my mouth might be better than the pain I'm causing myself trying to intercept it upstream.

If it were only the occasional concussion to worry about, I could live with the irksome consequences of water filtration. But it's not …

(I am reading now from the instructions for changing the filter.)

1. *Turn off incoming water supply before changing cartridge.*
2. *After relieving pressure in filter housing by pushing red vent button, unscrew housing and remove old cartridge.*
3. *Wash housing thoroughly with soap and water.*

Okay, I can handle this. I turn off the main and depressurize the housing by pressing the red vent button visible only to exceedingly tall people. Then I unscrew the housing and throw away the old cartridge.

My basement doesn't have a utility basin or powder room, so I bring the housing upstairs to the kitchen sink to wash it thoroughly with soap and water. Simple enough; all we're talking about here is a little sediment at the bottom. I've seen tea leaves more tenacious. I turn on the faucet.

"What's that sound?" I ask myself. "Could it be coming from the basement?" (Of course we don't actually talk that way, like characters on *Masterpiece Theater* inquiring, "Could it be Mistress Olivia who alerted the constable?")

I run to the basement. Water is erupting from the housing lid like a fire hydrant the neighborhood kids have opened illegally.

That red button depressurized the filter housing. It didn't do much for THE ENTIRE HOUSE! Miraculously, though, my expletives are now as clear as a teenager's skin on Accutane.

I run to check the main. It's turned off.

Back now at the water line breach, it's every submarine movie you've ever seen and I'm the crewman trying to stop the water that's spraying all over the place after the depth charges have gone off. Only, he knows what he's doing. The only thing I know is the pressure in my shower should be this good.

I tear back upstairs, where, in my panic, I left the kitchen sink running. Instinctively, I turn the faucet off, and the sound of a hundred fire hoses … goes … away.

Now I'm no expert on closed, pressurized systems (except for a few offices I've worked in), but shouldn't those instructions have said, "HAVE SOME WATER SET ASIDE FOR STEP 3 OR YOU'LL BE SORRY"?

Six months later, the now-brown filter whispers to me, "Hey, tall guy, aren't we about due?" Immediately, I remember my U-boat experience. Unfortunately, I can't remember what I did to cause it. Consequently, the same thing happens again.

Next week: *The BT24 and the Ice-Maker Filter Go for the Kill.*

SPORTS:
BASEBALL

It's mano-a-mano, a primal confrontation between a guy on a hill and a guy with a club.

The Duel

It's been hands-on baseball for me since mid-January, and I have to admit I'm ready for a break. The high school season segues right into Legion and travel ball with nary a moment to catch your breath. Practice started for my travel team in late April, and since then, my trunk has been stuffed with helmets, balls, bats and catcher's gear, and the car seats and floor smeared with dirt and the powdered residue of field lime.

Just when you think you've had enough, along comes a game that reminds you that baseball is anything but a languid pastime for languid summer nights. We played such a game two nights ago. How to begin describing the excruciating tension you're subjected to when your team is clinging to a lead in the last inning of a game to determine who makes the playoffs. It's a simultaneous yearning to be released and to never be released from the unbearable uncertainty of what's to come. If you're a baseball fan, you know the feeling.

The score is 6-4 and the other team has just loaded the bases with two outs in the bottom of the seventh, and potentially last, inning. All sorts of mayhem can happen in that situation, none of it good for my team. The umpire's strike zone has shrunk to the dimensions of a CD jewel box. The batter has worked the count to 3-2. He and the pitcher are engaged in a fascinating battle worthy of *Animal Kingdom*.

The pitcher is afraid to lose his rhythm by throwing too hard in an effort to blow the ball by the batter, and he's reluctant to throw his curve ball for fear of walking the batter. He has no choice but to keep putting fast balls in different parts of the now-shrunken strike zone – no easy feat. Meanwhile, the batter must get his bat on any pitch remotely close to the strike zone. He is in no position to let a close one go by in the hope that the umpire will call it ball four.

At three balls, two strikes with two outs, all three baserunners throw caution to the wind and are running as soon as the pitcher commits his motion to home plate. This is because if the next pitch is strike three, that's the third out and the inning is over, so no harm in running. If it's a ball, the batter walks, which forces the runners to advance one base anyway. And if the pitch is hit, the jump they get on the basepaths can result in the runner on first coming all the way around to score what would be, in this case, the winning run.

With the count 3-2, the batter has fouled off four straight pitches. This is not a sign of inferior hitting ability. Rather, this is an heroic, excellent at-bat. Every time he fouls one off, he increases the pitcher's odds of his next pitch being ball four. It puts extraordinary pressure on the pitcher. That young man is alone out there on the mound trying his hardest not to let his team down by walking the batter. A walk is so deflating to both him and the team. Not only does it bring the other team a run closer to tying the game, it also means the fielders must gird themselves again and refocus. More importantly, it means the pitcher must now throw even more pitches, when his arm is probably near exhaustion.

It's mano-a-mano, a primal confrontation between a guy on a hill and a guy with a club. The pitcher knows he has a good defense behind him, but a ball hit on the ground, or even in the air, can do funny things, and he'd rather get the job done himself, if possible. The batter, meanwhile, is trying to perform one of the hardest skills in all of sport: hit a ball moving at high speed with his swinging stick in a way that allows him to safely reach a base a mere 90 feet away while nine guys team up to stop him.

In the dugout, our stomachs are churning and our breathing is labored. All to a double-time heartbeat. There is no strategizing to engage in. All we can do is watch.

On the eleventh pitch of the at-bat, the batter pops one up between third and home. The third-baseman, catcher, and pitcher all converge. The catcher backs off when he realizes he must cover the plate. It's the pitcher who has the best angle, but we've coached the boys, now that they're older, that the pitcher should get out of the way and let his fielder make the catch. The baserunners are running as the ball rises and begins its descent. Our coaching fundamentals go out the window as our pitcher shouts louder than I've ever heard him shout, "I got it!" He watches the ball into his glove like a parent watching his child on stage, seeing nothing but the object of his affection. During the past two hours, this ball has been flung, struck, and thrown in the dirt, but now he cradles it as if reunited with a long-lost prodigal, determined never again to let it go. Yes, it's he who makes the catch for the final out – deservedly so.

The release from this gut-wrenching drama is exquisite. We burst out onto the field, smiles as broad as a throw from third to first. In true baseball tradition, we pummel our pitcher, who has had a character-building experience that will serve him his lifetime.

All my bone-weariness and mental fatigue is wiped away in the glory of the moment, and I am renewed.

Can you tell?

We read almost daily how lacrosse is becoming increasingly popular among today's youth -- at baseball's expense. As a baseball man, I'm distressed by this.

Lacrosse vs. Baseball: No Contest

So I revved up my search engine to marshal some good counter-arguments against this Johnny-come-not-so-lately sport that originated with the Native Americans. Over the years, famous literary pieces and comedy routines by the likes of Tom Boswell and George Carlin have explored the contrasts between baseball and football, but I found nothing pitting baseball against lacrosse.

That leaves it to me -- baseball coach and writer – to get the balls rolling. I offer then this modest list of The *Top Ten Reasons Why Baseball Is Better Than Lacrosse:*

> 10. Unlike lacrosse (LAX), baseball is not easily confused with the Los Angeles International Airport (LAX).
>
> 9. When lacrosse is televised (wherever that is), have you seen any fan in the stands exultantly displaying the foul lacrosse ball he's caught?
>
> 8. Aesthetically, what does a lacrosse field offer us that's any different from a soccer field? Both are bland, green rectangles differentiated only by where their circles and lines are painted. Wait, I forgot the corner flags.
>
> 7. Corollary to reason #8: Is there a prettier field of play in all of sport than a baseball diamond at game time?
>
> 6. We already have five back-and-forth sports in football, basketball, ice hockey, soccer, and rugby. If it weren't for baseball, we'd have no team ball sports that *aren't* of the this-end / that-end variety. Oh, I forgot tennis doubles.

5. Only baseball offers the tactile and meditative pleasures each game of lining the batter's box and grooming the pitcher's mound.

4. The deception in lacrosse is one-dimensional. Faked shots, give-and-go, and backdoor cuts – things that are common to all the back-and-forth sports. But good baseball deception, with its intricate system of signs and timing plays, is like a master magician's sleight of hand. It leaves you wondering: How'd they do that? (Author's addendum: Of course with the Astros, now we know!)

3. Has lacrosse yet produced a classic to match the incomparable "Who's On First?" What … "Who's in the Wing Area?"

2. Will a lacrosse ball ever soar as high as a towering fly ball?

And finally, the #1 Reason Why Baseball Is Better Than Lacrosse:

1. In lacrosse, the focal point on the field is the goal, which is a perfect six-by-six-foot square. (I'm already getting sleepy just typing that description.) What happens to that goal? Not much. Lacrosse balls go into it, like soccer balls into soccer nets and hockey pucks into hockey nets. Baseball's focal point, on the other hand, is home plate. Like homes and plates everywhere, it fosters disputes and regularly gets dirty. It is stepped on, slid across, and brushed clean. Paradoxically, it is struck by balls but not struck by strikes. Its dimensions and angles (most definitely not *square*) dictate what is fair and what is foul, and what is a strike and what is not -- giving it great jurisdiction over players' actions, like a court of law.

So, if you had to choose between a lacrosse goal and a home plate, is there any question which one you'd ask to the prom?

I rest my case.

Hey, sportswriter. Get your nuances straight.

Questionable Reporting on the Fly

When *Gazette* columnist Steve Sherman reported in his 5/27 article on the recent New Hope-Solebury Varsity-Alumni baseball game that I'd "booted a few balls in the process" of playing the field, my first impulse was to write a letter to the editor demanding a retraction.

Then I realized, hey, I write a column.

So here's what really happened.

Yes, I was playing for my team since we were short of players, and, yes, I did drop a ball while playing first base. But where Steve dropped his own ball was in his missing the nuances that made the act almost an Herculean achievement.

Consider this: In the moments leading up to the actual miscatch (I prefer that word to "error"), I had successfully navigated a task that confounds and – let's not mince words here – *injuries* lesser athletes than myself. I'm talking about backpedaling. Do you know what an act of faith it is for a middle-aged man with cartilage-shredded knees to backpedal on clumpy grass with his neck craned back and his eyes looking up at nothing but sky and a spinning cowhide sphere? But does Sherman award me any points on the courage meter for that effort? No. One of the alumni players, himself now aware that his best years are long behind him, recognized the magnitude of my achievement by telling me, "Hey, you got under it at least."

How hard is it to catch a popup when you're into the late innings of the second game of the doubleheader that is your life? Well, a fellow (old) coach who'd come down with a three-month case of vertigo told me that his neurologist told him the best test for determining if you've gotten over the condition is to be able to catch a popup. "All that vectoring you have to do." Yet there I was, backpedaling and vectoring, proving to the world that the only vertigo in my life was the Hitchcock film I have at home on videocassette. And just about to squeeze that ball for the third out when it hit off the heel of my glove and fell to the ground.

Let's talk about that glove for a minute. Do you think I would have dropped that ball had I been properly equipped with a first-baseman's glove? No way. But all I had was my son's top-of-the-line Wilson A2000 pitcher's glove. At 11 ¾ inches from the tip of the middle finger to the bottom of the heel, it's no match for a longer, first baseman's mitt.

But, John, you counter, shortstops and second basemen use *ten-inch* gloves, yet they catch high pops all the time.

Yeah, well, do they have to worry about coaching the game at the same time? You try coaching and catching at the same time. And with no wind blowing. You see, I had already factored in a right-handed batter's slice on balls hit to the opposite field. But my mental calculations didn't take into consideration the still weather conditions we were experiencing.

Fielders often remark how hard it is to catch a ball in the sun, but there's an art to catching a ball with the sun to your back as well. Steve Sherman probably forgot that in his reporting.

So, have we established that the ball I dropped would've probably been scored a hit in a real game? Good. Now, to correct Steve's inaccurate description of me booting "a few balls." He was obviously mistaking me for someone else (and, by the way, that high throw that got by me was scored an error on the third baseman, or would have been if one of my players had been keeping the scorebook). And, contrary to what Steve reported, I was never in left field, though I'm flattered that he mistook me for the sophomore we had playing there. I played two innings in *right* field, where I caught the only ball hit my way. It was a fly ball I had to run a significant distance in a forward direction to catch, forcefully calling off Pat Moore, my assistant coach, at the last second. Pat, who reports to me, will attest both to my calling for the ball and to the athleticism of the catch itself, which I made Willie Mays basket-catch style, though not intentionally. I am not a showboat.

In two fielding chances, then, I demonstrated an ability to go both backward and forward. That is statistically significant.

Maybe Steve was confusing me with Donald Becker, the *Gazette*'s staff photographer, who is six inches shorter and THIRTY YEARS YOUNGER! than I. Donald, whose name is to Steely Dan as Allen wrenches are to IKEA, was there to take pictures but got conscripted into playing centerfield for our varsity team. It's a good thing those baseballs he dropped weren't camera lenses.

Rather than focusing on the perfectly justifiable miscues of the New Hope-Solebury baseball coach, who, as I've just demonstrated, was probably one of the stars of the game, maybe Steve Sherman should use his writing powers to persuade his paper to hold more infield-outfield practice for its staff. You never know when they'll be asked to suit up.

I'm not even going to attempt to be funny in this introduction.

When Hitting Instruction Isn't Part of the Job Description

As a baseball coach, I struggle to express how strongly I feel about having Mark Downs Jr. of Dunbar, Fayette County as a fellow member of our great sport's coaching fraternity. Mark is taking some heat these days, but every sport needs young coaches with exciting new strategies for achieving success on the playing field. In that respect, Mark's recent actions transcend anything that's gone before.

Some youth-sport coaches just go through the motions, but Mark Downs Jr. approaches the business of coaching and molding young, impressionable minds with passion and purpose. How much passion? So much that, according to a recent AP press release, he was arrested and charged with paying one of his tee-ball players $25 to hit an autistic teammate in the head with a baseball so that the coach – that would be Mark – wouldn't have to put the boy in the game.

Tactically, this was a brilliant maneuver in that it would allow Mark to circumvent his league's rule requiring each player to participate in three innings a game. Rules like that only tie the hands of creative coaches like Mark Downs Jr.

Police said the boy was hit in the head and the groin with a baseball just before the game and didn't play. For this, local authorities charged Downs with corruption of minors and criminal solicitation to commit aggravated assault.

But wasn't Mark just fulfilling his role as a skill developer? After all, isn't "hitting instruction" a big part of baseball? And how about throwing accuracy? Mark must be doing something right. It's not easy to aim for the head and the groin and actually hit them.

I do have one concern, however. It was reported that Mark had two daughters on his tee-ball team, but it was not stated whether one of them was the player to whom he paid the $25. That would be overstepping some ethical bound, I'd think. Now we'd be talking nepotism, and nobody likes it when relatives profit by their connection to those in power.

What a problem it must have been for my fellow coach. There he was, trying to win the tee-ball championship of his local youth baseball league, and he's stuck with a mentally disabled player on his team. Although the boy was eight years old and probably towered over his younger teammates, what tee-ball coach wouldn't want to shed that baggage? How could such a player hope to match the fielding, throwing, and baserunning brilliance of the five- and six-year-olds on his team? If you've ever seen a tee-ball game, you know what I mean. The skill set of tee-ballers is impressive, even to the untrained eye.

Why, I've seen some tee-ball outfielders turn cartwheels while the ball's in play. Others are able to crane their necks in all directions, even as the ball is coming right at them. Some are even able to turn their backs on the play taking place in their own game to watch a game going on elsewhere.

But the most impressive are those who have the Zen-like ability to tune out the game entirely, from start to finish. Now that's detachment.

But from the autistic child, what was the best that Mark Downs Jr. could expect? The enjoyment of participating? A grin a mile wide? The thrill of catching a ball or getting a hit? (Not to be confused with getting hit.)

No, that's not what wins championships.

Or is it?

Take it from a fellow coach, Mark. You can't please everybody. You do what it takes to win, and if it means hurting the feelings – and, all right, the body – of a child to achieve your ends, so be it. Ty Cobb took no prisoners, and he's in the Hall of Fame.

Now you're headed for the Hall yourself. The Hall of Shame.

SPORTS:
NON-BASEBALL

Where "tight end" takes on a whole new meaning.

Hash Marks, Yes; Stretch Marks, Never

I'm trying to get my arms around the new Lingerie Football League – and any of the women who play in it. My last attraction to women in a league of their own was at a movie theater. Rosie O'Donnell, Madonna and Geena Davis were flashing some serious leather, better than the Dominatrix League even. It aroused me no end. But that's because I'm a baseball fan.

Our local LFL franchise is the Philadelphia Passion, and isn't that a great name for a sports team, you're thinking, until you see teams in the league with names like Seduction, Temptation and Caliente and begin to get the picture.

The Tampa Breeze and the Seattle Mist, two other Lingerie League entries, seem to have missed that it's not about the weather.

This is a soft-porn league, after all, and the backers are hoping that the kind of spectator who pays to watch two women mud wrestle will pay even more to watch 14 of them block and tackle.

Not that they have experience blocking and tackling. In fact, none of the girls had prior football experience before signing with the Passion. But so what? Did Edison work for G.E. before he invented the light bulb?

The league's inaugural season runs 20 weeks, from September 4 to January 29. That coincides with the NFL's season almost to the day, excluding the Super Bowl. So far, it doesn't look as if there's going to be an LFL Super Bowl, though. This may have to do with the four-game schedule the girls play. In a 20-week season, that's a game every five weeks. Not much of a grind, except in a certain sense.

If they ever do hold their own Super Bowl, they'll need a different name for it anyway.

Super Cup, maybe.

Ticket prices for the Passion's home games range from $15 to $105. They are adult only. The $105 seats are first-row lower level, so close to the action that you could get yourself an inadvertent lap dance on a basic out pattern.

But let's talk about the uniforms for a second, starting with the eye black that every player wears. God, that's so hot!

An LFL player's uniform is – what's the word I'm looking for that means "even the Hubbell telescope couldn't locate it?" – scanty. In a nod to safety, it includes a set of shoulder pads and a hockey helmet. No hip pads, however. Though bodies often hit the ground in lingerie football – taut, sensuous bodies writhing in flesh-pressed piles, I might add – protective hip pads would detract from the visual element of booty shorts clinging seductively to expressive pelvises.

And that's a problem.

So is the one the Lingerie Football League designers ran into with the players' uniform numbers. Athletes in team sports become identified with the number on the back of their jerseys – Michael Jordan and 23, for example. But what's a pole-dancer-turned-QB to do when her jersey is a plunging, ribbon-accented sports bra covered by shoulder pads?

The designers – God bless 'em – solved that one by putting players' numbers on their right butt cheeks.

Right now, I'm admiring that inspired move here at my local sports bra … bar … as I watch the Seduction and Temptation go at it on pay-per-view. The uniform numbers are smaller on the butt than they'd be on the back of a jersey, so spectators have to work a little harder to read them. (Precisely.) But the off-center design leaves the left cheek unadorned, in all its pristine, curvaceous loveli … sorry.

The Passion are 1-1 so far, with the season more than half over. If they can manage to avoid injuries, hip pointers in particular, they can finish 3-1, and that just might be enough to give Philadelphia the football championship it deserves.

Arm bars, guillotine chokes, ground and pounds. What ever happened to the good old half nelson?

The Next Great American Spectacle?

Herb is 73, and there's nothing he enjoys more these days than getting Stanley, his fellow retiree, in an inescapable guillotine choke. Aside from his forearms, Herb holds nothing against Stan personally, something he delights in reminding him as the headlock pinches the blood flow to Stan's brain. If Stan doesn't tap out soon and submit, in a few moments he'll be unconscious, but not before wondering how the heck Herb managed to slip out of the arm bar he had him in a minute ago.

America, welcome to the next great Baby Boomer recreational activity: Mixed Martial AARPs.

(Or, as the ring announcer might say, "L ... L ... Let's get ready to crumble.")

Haven't heard of Mixed Martial AARPs yet? You will someday. Take my word.

Just about every other sport has its "senior division." Seniors play golf and tennis. They bowl and swim, play bocce ball, basketball and softball. They row. They probably even luge and surf. Why not mixed martial arts?

"Wait a minute, Shields," you're thinking. "You haven't displayed an iota of interest in martial arts until the day you began writing this column, so what's going on?"

Let me give you the run-up.

Three Decembers ago, my son Nick, then a college sophomore and acknowledged video gamer, told me he'd like the soon-to-be-released Nintendo Wii for Christmas.

"It's going to rule the market," he said after I reminded him that, by all accounts, Nintendo at the time was toast.

Of course the Wii went on to do just what Nick said it would, and the minute I rolled my first frame of its interactive bowling game that Christmas, I knew it was going to be a generational crossover hit, something my son had foreseen months earlier. From then on, I knew not to question his judgment about cultural developments unknown to me.

Flush with I-told-you-so success, Nick must've felt himself on a mission, because soon afterward he asked me to watch something on cable TV called "Pride Fighting."

A documentary about lions?

A form of LGBTQ self-expression?

It was neither. Instead, it looked something like professional wrestling, that is to say, buff guys and pre-ordained outcomes.

Only it wasn't.

The spectacle we were watching is called "K-1." It's a combat sport played out in a ring, like pro wrestling, but that's where the similarity ends. K-1 combines techniques from karate, tae kwondo, ju jitsu, and something called Muay Thai, the national sport of Thailand. Add kickboxing and regular boxing and there you have it: mixed martial arts, or MMA.

I know, I thought Muay Thai was a mixed drink, too. But it's a martial art that allows the use of elbows and knees for striking.

(In Mixed Martial AARPs, they would be for support.)

The object of K-1 tournaments is to determine the best stand-up fighter in the world, and, from the looks of things, that meant the fighter still standing up when it was over. Watching what these guys were doing to each other made "brutal" sound like a champagne review. Yet Nick assured me that this three-round sport is far less punishing than regular boxing because there are so many fewer head blows.

That may be, but what about that last elbow to the Adam's apple?

(Mixed Martial AARPs acknowledges that the pointy elbows of many of its combatants' pose a health risk. Therefore, any elbow that breaks either the skin or the artificial voice box of an opponent will result in a mandatory $20 increase to his Medicare Part B premium.)

At first, I thought Pride Fighting was just another tawdry concoction to keep cable going 24 / 7. But after watching a few bouts, I began to appreciate the multi-faceted athleticism these fighters possessed.

So there I was one Saturday night, alone in my living room ... watching an MMA match on – ready for this? – network television. The event attracted 4.56 million viewers, according to CBS, making it the top-rated show for males ages 18-34, beating out every major league baseball playoff and college football game that week.

Nick, you called it again.

As I was watching Seth Petruzelli knock out Kimbo Slice (the latter looking like an indigenous Australian nightclub bouncer), the wheels began to turn. This could be a new boom. A Boomer boom. Sure, there'd be neurologic and orthopedic waivers to be signed and spandex modifications to be made. But what an upside! ...

Stanley, meanwhile, has slipped Herb's guillotine choke after Herb's arthritis suddenly flared up *and* he couldn't remember where he was, and now Stan's inflicting the old ground-and-pound on his septuagenarian adversary and ... there it is! ... Herb taps out! Herb has tapped out! We have a submission, and it's not a screenplay! It's ...

... M-I-X-E-D ... M-A-R-T-I-A-L ... A-A-R-P-S ...!

I grew up in the inner city. Many of my neighbors did not. Here's one way you can tell.

Volunteering for the Chain Gang

Today in the suburbs, Johnny, age 11 and the youngest of my three children, asked if we could replace our basketball net with a chain one.

If you're a person with an affinity for irony, or the city, or both, you'll appreciate that one. I grew up in the city – in Swampoodle, to be precise. Twentieth and Lehigh, across from the old Connie Mack Stadium. I played a lot of schoolyard basketball, most of it at two locales – Peirce Public School at 23rd and Cambria, and Whittier Playground at 27th and Clearfield, ten blocks from my home. I didn't mind the walk to Whittier because the baskets there had chain nets.

The baskets at Peirce, where I did most of my playing, didn't have nets. Shooting at a basket with no net makes for a disputatious sporting event:

"That was in."

"No, it wasn't; it was under."

In, under, over – with no net, they're *all* air balls, so what's the difference.

But at Whittier... *chungh.* When a jumper dropped cleanly through, there was no mistaking the sound.

My friend Tom contends that a chain net ruins a basketball by wearing away the pebbles until you're left with a smooth ball you can't control. I wouldn't know; I never had a ball good enough to notice it had gone bad.

At Peirce you were limited to a halfcourt game. There was no court as such, just two baskets side by side, their backboards bolted directly into the brick wall of the school. One was a foot higher than the other, with the 11-foot basket being the losers' court. Between them, at one of the doors leading into the building, was a granite landing step. There were certain fundamental skills you had to master to play the game successfully at Peirce, and caroming off the wall when you drove the lane was prominent among them. Dribbling up onto the landing to launch a jumper from the corner was another.

Add the absence of nets to such non-traditional court features and you can appreciate how a kid might venture farther afield in search of courts where the sound and the word were one: swish. Chain nets like the ones at Whittier were better than no nets at all, of course, but the Elysian Fields of city basketball courts were those with regulation, white-cord nets.

You cannot prove by me that such places existed.

Oh, once or twice I played at courts where the fossilized strands of what once could have been a real net hung in tatters from the rim. But the life span of a cord net in the city is about that of a light bulb in the stairway of a housing project. So, if you were a city kid, you resigned yourself to the fact that never the twine shall you meet.

And that's one of the reasons you moved to the suburbs first chance you got.

In the development where I live, the ratio of backboards to kids gives new meaning to the phrase "one-on-one." In driveway after driveway, baskets sprout from the ground like fiberglass sunflowers. Their nets are pristine, nylon 12-mesh, and there's not a rim that doesn't have one. If – not when – they rip, they are…replaced. Some have E-Z-return flaps attached so little Tyler doesn't have to fetch the ball after he makes a basket. Kids shoot at their baskets alone, or in small groups of two or three. The baskets can be raised or lowered to foster the self-esteem of kids of all sizes, each of whom has a ball with non-eroded pebbles. They don't have to fight to hold the court, because they own the court. In winter, they get to use gyms and play full court games, coached in the fundamentals by fathers who prove the dictum: We teach what we wish to learn.

Johnny knows what chain nets stand for – city ball. And if he wants some of that to rub off on him, he has my support. I'll even refuse to buy him a new ball when the chain's rubbed this one clean.

SELF

I can't even find the aisle, let alone the balm.

Balms Away

Monday, Dec. 4th

Dear diary,

Confusion on the toiletries front.

Ran out of my Nivea for Men Mild Balm after-shave. Went to CVS for more. Got there and remembered Nivea but couldn't remember what degree of balm I had.

There's a word for that sort of behavior: frequent.

"Cooling Balm?" No. That had menthol. I haven't liked menthol since I tried Kools when I was 12.

"Replenishing Balm." That might be it.

Wait a sec. Here's Replenishing Balm with a built-in dispenser for the same price. What to do, diary?

Professor Buck, Econ 401, always said, "Make your decisions at the margin."

Would the dispenser be more convenient than twisting the cap off and on every day? Yes, but what if it dripped? What if it clogged? Then I'm stuck until I run out again.

And what if Replenishing Balm isn't the kind I had at home? Should I risk buying it? Then what? Return it when it turns out not to be? Now we're talking gas and wear and tear.

I *could* use it liberally every time I shave, but that would get me in the habit of using it liberally every time I shave – just what Nivea wants me to do. I will not be manipulated that way, diary.

Do I really need a dispenser for after-shave? I decide I don't. I play it safe and buy the Replenishing Balm with the regular cap. Now I'm happy with myself. I drive home.

It's the wrong balm.

Tuesday, Dec. 5th

Dear diary,

Before I go on, diary, I have to change your name to "journal." People have been asking questions. Sorry.

A routine morning. Showered with my Sensory Fusion Body Wash, then lathered up my whiskers with Gillette Fusion HydraGel and shaved them off with my Fusion razor. (While shaving, thought about how hard it would be to shave the Hydra. Nine moving heads. That's six more than a Norelco.)

Followed this with a liberal splash of Nivea Replenishing Balm.

Got dressed then grabbed my usual morning meal: toast and a glass of V8 Fusion. Brushed my teeth with Mentadent Peppermint Fusion toothpaste and headed out.

Hopped into my Ford Fusion for the morning commute and turned on my usual: 108.3 FM, the jazz-fusion station.

Quiet day at the office, but lunch was a treat, journal. Ate at the Seoul Delhi, my favorite new fusion cuisine restaurant. The menu is Indian-Korean-African American-Jewish. I had the kimchi with a side of cornbread and collard greens served kosher on a bed of nails. Almost as delicious as the Southwest-Cuban fusion dishes at Havana Gila.

Wednesday, Dec. 6th

Dear journal,

Will not be replenishing the Replenishing Balm. Not sure what, exactly, it replenished. Decided not to wait until I used it up. Wrote "MILD BALM" on my palm so I wouldn't forget it again and went shopping for it. Found it at Whisker World in the Imported Organic Toiletry section.

I'm not throwing out my unused Replenishing Balm, though. No, I'm mixing it with the Mild Balm to make my own special after-shave: Mildly Replenishing Fusion Balm.

A gnawing guilt has been – what else? – gnawing at me. "Nah," you say, "no reason to feel ashamed. It was the nun's fault." You, the reader, can be the judge.

IQ Fraud

My name is John, and I'm an IQ fraud.

(*Hello, John.*)

Not a decade goes by that I don't think about that and its impact on friends, loved ones, casual acquaintances, total strangers, foreigners, resident aliens, statisticians, and, yes, my classmates from St. Columba Parochial School.

I've been in denial about it all these years. Now it's time to be honest, if only with myself.

I recall it as if it were yesterday …

It was the big day, the day when Sister Lucretia Borgia handed out the Stanford-Binet IQ test to her class of seventh-grade boys. She counseled us pointedly (by jabbing her pointer into the nearby chest of woeful William Wacker) that cheating on the test was for-*bid*-den.

"You'll look stupider or smarter than you really are," she said, instantly creating an incentive program for half the class.

Perhaps sensing that, she gave us a disincentive to consider, namely, that to be caught cheating would result in the usual shit kicking from her in the coatroom.

She may not have used those words exactly.

Sister Lucretia had the all-boys class because she was a fierce disciplinarian with Mike Tyson-like punching power, the most devastating of any nun in St. Columba school ("columba" meaning "dove" in Latin).

My theory is that I was put into her classroom to toughen me up, get me to be one of the guys. Until then, I'd always been in mixed classrooms of boys and girls, where I was a model student – obedient, neat, and hygienic.

I attribute my perfect behavior to my stature as The Smartest Kid in Class. As such, I always occupied the "first row, first seat," a dubious honor conferred upon the brainiest pupil in the room. It's hard to get into trouble from there. All the action is behind you.

You're probably wondering, then, what made me cheat on my IQ test with those credentials?

Another nun put me up to it.

Her name was Sister Anne Joseph.

She was my aunt, my mother's oldest sister, but no one in the family called her "Aunt Sister Anne Joseph." It was hard enough figuring out why she had a guy's name let alone introduce a Mormon component into it.

A teacher herself, Sister Anne Joseph had access to the Stanford-Binet. On the weekend before the official test in school, she pulled me away from playing with my cousins and administered the test to me in my dining room at home.

I think it was to give me some practice ahead of time. Why else would she do it, with the real deal only days away? Something about it didn't seem nun-like or the Catholic thing to do, but at age 12 and obedient as a trained seal, was I going to take a moral stand?

I never learned what score I achieved on this unofficial test, but it helped me take the official one with something akin to a veteran's preference.

I scored 134.

Mensa territory, I came to find out.

There's more.

In the seat directly behind me that day was Robert Gibson. Robert was a slow-witted, lanky, freckled kid. Never said much. Everything about him looked slightly Appalachian. He was one of those tall guys that were always assigned the last seat in the row so they wouldn't block anyone's view of the blackboard.

Gibson happened to be sitting behind me because Sister Lucretia had moved kids around for the test to deter cheating. By that measure, *I* should've been in the last seat. My front-seat location invited cheating eyes, and, as I saw it, part of my "one-of-the-guys" training was to oblige them.

Thus, I accommodated the special needs of my deluded classmate, who must've thought that stealing IQ-test answers would help his report card.

Robert Gibson may have been deficient in other areas of his life, but eyesight was not one of them.

He wound up with the second highest IQ in the class.

How do I know that? Because Sister Lucretia, in her pedagogic wisdom, seated us for the rest of the school year according to our IQ rankings.

Gibson acquired the nickname "Stretch" shortly after the new seat assignments, and he went on to become chairman and CEO of a major educational testing service, after making his first fortune right out of Harvard as a pioneer in the field of office ergonomics. The dedication of his best-selling autobiography, *Location Is Everything*, reads

For JS, one of the guys

As for Sister Anne Joseph, she didn't do me any favors. My IQ is in question, Mensa has demoted me to Condimensa, and I hear that Sister Lucretia's still tracking me down.

It's enough to keep a guy up at night, I swear.

Mi Stressa Es Su Stressa

By and large, I'm asleep at night a minute after the pillow and my head begin foreplay – about the same as my wife's timetable back in the day. All it takes is a good, shoulders-back, belly-forward, lower-back stretch and a moment or two to locate the proper comfort angle for my arm and I'm out faster than a pinch-hitter facing Mariano Rivera.

But there are nights – you've had them – when the mind takes over and I'm hostage to the pressing concerns it deposits into my mental in-basket.

Perhaps you've dwelt on these, too.

Is it cheaper to rotate your tires every 7,000 miles or never rotate them and just buy new ones when they wear out?

I was a rotating zealot. A whirling dervish of tire maintenance. Then one night, lying in bed, I asked myself: Is it worth paying my mechanic twice a year to rotate my tires? For the $80 it's costing me to rotate each year, the money I'd save over the useful life of a set of tires would just about pay for new tires.

Until I work out the math in my head, though, I'm lying there counting the number of rpms on my ceiling fan.

What is the best combination of keyboard symbols to suggest a swear word?

Okay, this is a writer's concern, I'll admit. But, to answer the question, I don't think stringing four or five of them consecutively really cuts it, and it's a lazy approach besides.

"Who forgot to put out the !@#$% trash?"

See what I mean? Not bad, but I think that exclamation point needs to be at the end. Maybe even repeated, for emphasis.

A few years ago I wrote a piece about modern-day packaging and invented a company called "@!!&%#! No More." That was pretty good, but I see now that I never should have included the "@." What did that add (heh heh)?

See how this line of thinking might drive a frustrated sleeper to scream bloody #*!%& murder? (New curse-word substitution rule: never place a percent sign and an ampersand next to each other. Too many loops.)

Why doesn't everyone have E-ZPass?

When this thought pops into my head at night and keeps me awake, I try counting cars waiting in line to pay their tolls.

The #&~*! service is FREE, people! You can't tell me that everyone waiting in the Cash Only lines needs a receipt. Maybe they get a rush from producing Exact Change in the nick of time.

Tip for the E-ZPassless: When you do finally acquire, first, a brain and, next, an E-ZPass transponder, don't do what I did and request a monthly statement. That *will* cost you, to the tune of $4.00 a month, basically to see which toll plazas you've visited.

(The tilde (~), by the way, is rarely seen in a swear-symbol word, and, in the above example, you can see why.)

Which would you rather have: no privacy, or one more HIPAA privacy form?

At 3:44 in the morning with a ceiling fan rpm of 140 per minute, I'd gladly forego my right to privacy in exchange for the promise that I'll never receive a single one of those *%^&!# forms again. (Don't worry about neglecting either the tilde or the caret (^) when constructing your own swear-symbol words. Both are just too friendly and clearly need to be excluded.)

What precise minute constitutes "the dead of night?"

This is a very subjective question, I know. I also know that, whichever minute it is, it usually passes while I'm lying awake thinking about it. For my money, it's 3:44 a.m. Then again, 4:01 is right up there. Or maybe it's

3:39. ... I'm sorry I even brought this up. It will stick with you like a bad credit report.

Is Arthur Kaplan the only bioethicist in America?

If not, how come he's the only one they ever quote when they need a genome or feeding tube comment? I wonder what he knows about tire rotation? Or HIPAA?

So you can see my sleep hours are often just as fraught with worry as yours are. But what the %&-^@ do I care?

Call me thrifty, but I like to get the most – and I mean the most – out of the things I buy.

When Terrycloth Gets Threadbare, I've Done My Job

Yesterday evening brought that first taste of autumn to the air after a muggy summer. The temperature was in the 50s, chilly enough for me to reach into my closet for the warmth of a sweater.

Most were still in summer storage, but I always keep my favorite for immediate access year-round. I bought it in Halifax on a four-day family cruise out of New York. It's a collared, two-button pullover and loose fitting, which is just the way I like it. All it says on it is "Nova Scotia," embroidered but unobtrusive, which is also just the way I like it. I'm not one to donate my torso to clothing manufacturers for free advertising. Branding is for cattle, though tell that to the bovine community.

Like most males, I don't need much in the way of a wardrobe, and I'm quite content to wear favorite items for years. I have a tee shirt from Lenny & Joe's Fishtale Restaurant in Westbrook, Connecticut – one merchant I *will* advertise; what a lobster roll! – that I bought in 1985. I wore it regularly until about three years ago, when I had to stop. It had gotten so threadbare that sections would just blow off in the wind. That's alright, though. My teenage son John still wears it to bed.

He gets it.

Towels fall into this category, too. A towel is built to last from bridal shower to grave. I'll hold onto one unless it's been somewhere so fetid and objectionable that its condition is hopeless – my son's car, for example.

My penchant for sartorial stagnation and timeless terrycloth didn't sit well with my ex-wife. And I guess I can't blame her. Sex isn't the only place where you have to have a little variation from time to time.

I should add cars to that list. If we were still driving the same car eight years later, one of us was not happy. Guess which?

You've probably also figured out by now that I'm not much of a shopper either, another area where my wife and I butted lifestyles. For her, shopping was an aphrodisiac, which is why I'd quick throw a bottle of chardonnay into the fridge whenever she'd call me from the mall.

Maryland crabs were *my* aphrodisiac – the dirtier the better. (Here again the sex analogy.) But she was allergic to crabs.

Are you sensing a pattern here?

But I digress; shellfish is not today's topic.

My habit of getting the most out of my possessions was born out of the travel experience I had when I was a young man, when I went halfway around the world for nine months – a second birth in a very real sense – and learned just how little one really needs. The items I cherish the most resonate not only with personal significance but with useful longevity, like the Martin guitar I bought for myself with an income tax refund back when I was single – a million or so strums ago.

I try not to be one of those people who use shopping as an antidote to depression. They'd do better smoking crack cocaine. Shopping gives you the quick high, sure, but with crack, at least, you don't have to return anything or find a parking space at the mall the weekend before Christmas. And you never have to call technical support -- unless it's an EMT).

With recent economic developments, however, the days of shopping-as-Ecstasy may be over. If a $700 billion bailout doesn't prompt a move toward saving more and owing less, I don't know what will. And maybe even that won't. We're a nation of borrowers and spenders, looking for the kind of quick gratification shopping and buying can provide.

But how will that behavior fare in the New Economy post-September 19th? I believe we'll be looking to a certain type of individual for guidance through the dark days to come.

The type who still uses the towels he got on his wedding day in 1983.

The type who can stretch his contact lens solution six months beyond the expiration date.

The type whose bars of soap celebrate anniversaries.

Yes, an individual who puts the "old" in "same old" and the "bla" in "bland." Someone perfectly suited for these apoco-nomic, econo-lyptic times. Someone whose time, at long last, has come.

I accept your nomination.

POETRY III

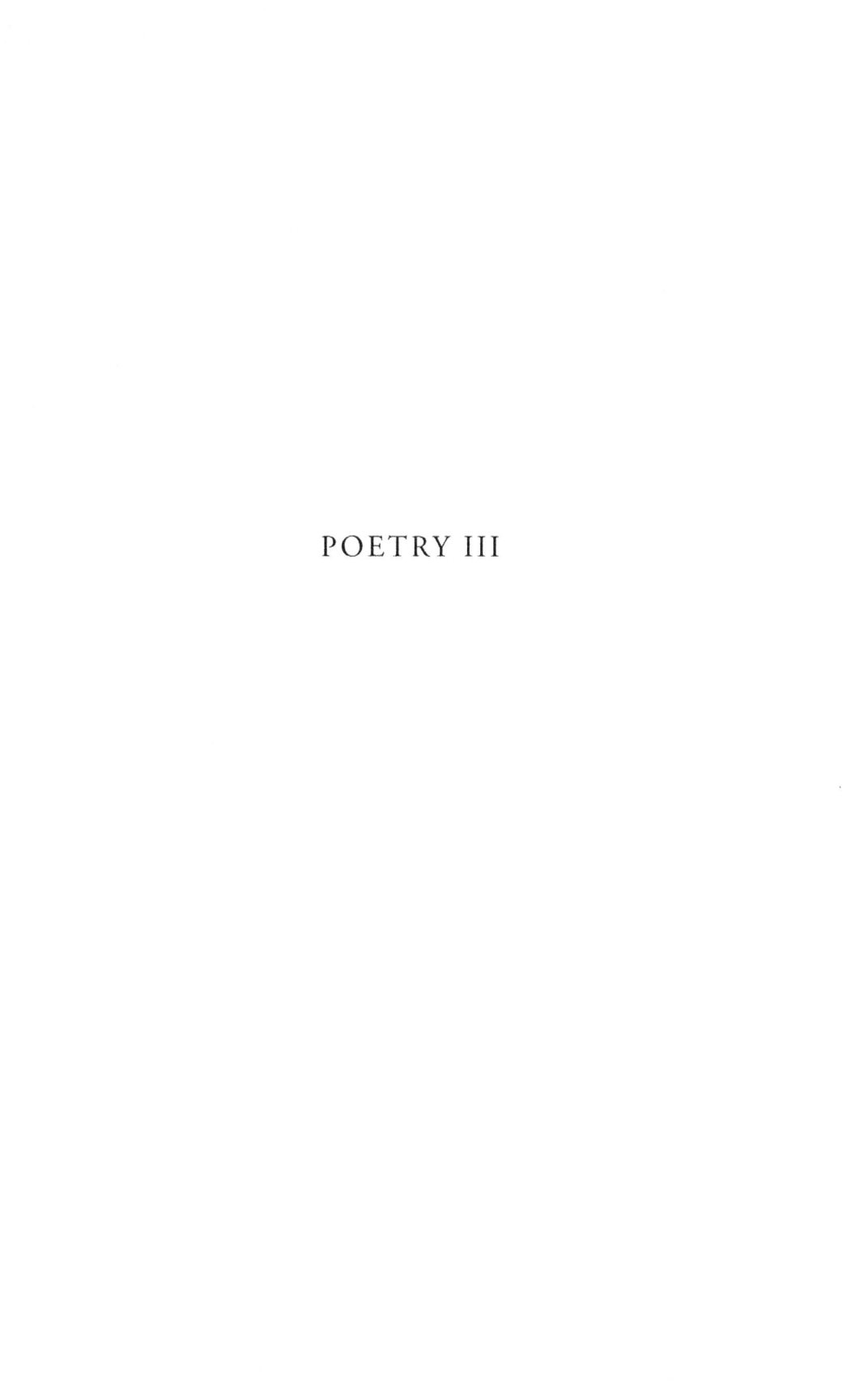

You probably remember those missing-child flyers that would populate your mailbox. Did anyone ever do anything but toss them right into the trash? Yes. Me.

Poetry: Could It Be Verse?

I was about to throw out my latest missing-child junk mail when something made me read what was on the other side.

(This is often how the Muse visits us artists – via direct mailing.)

Poetry – the International Library of Poetry, to be precise – was back in my life!

Two years ago, I was named a finalist in Poetry.com's annual contest for my submission entitled *I Am a Dad with Adult A.D.D.* When I declined their offer to include my verse in their commemorative volume, *Star Dust In The Morning,* I assumed that *I Am a Dad...* would be trashed faster than a two-line haiku, shredded more thoroughly than the cabbage in an obsessive-compulsive's coleslaw recipe.

But my piece of junk mail inspired me to return to the Poetry.com website, where I discovered that my poem remains in their collection – along with the works of a select group of 5.1 million other poets.

Verse's version of McDonald's hamburger count.

Not only is the website a portal to 5.1 million published poets, it's a resource for the aspiring, unpublished poet, too. Choose from links such as "POETIC TECHNIQUES," "NEED HELP RHYMING?" and "$150,000 MORTGAGE AS LOW AS $594/MO. RATES STILL LOW!"

I think it was Archibald MacLeish who said, "A poem must not mean, but be." (Or was it Mister Rogers saying, "A poem must not be mean?")

The fog of years never lifts / Like a longshoreman with a hernia.)

No matter. The mailer informs me that there will be 1,175 prizes awarded totaling $58,000. That's $49.36 per prize, but using the poetic technique of *hyperbole*, I will call it $50.

Directly beneath the prize-money announcement, I see there's another popular poetic technique at work: alliteration.

Possible publication!

I can see how the International Library of Poetry might not want to make guarantees. Poetry is not high school bowling, where everyone who comes out makes the team.

Still, with 5.1 million poets on their website, I don't think you'd be going out on a limb if you read that as

Probable publication!

Well, it's every poet for himself, so good luck to you, and may the best 50,000 win. I call my poem *Resident 337 Loller Rd Hatboro PA 19040*, and I dedicate it to Calliope, the Muse of epic poetry and direct marketing.

> My name is Jillian Haber
> My age is only 1
> At 2'3", you'd notice me
> If I were on the run.
> I'm not, but someone took me
> Her photo's to your right
> We've not been seen since 8/05
> And both of us are white
> Beth (the lady next to me) and I
> Have lt. brown hair
> Our eyes are blue, our sex is F
> We could be anywhere.
> Beth is kind of tall and lean
> 115 5'7"
> Me? I'm 20 pounds and chubby
> Thanks to 7-11.
> We hail from WI, right next to MI

I don't know what that means
But Beth says we're the Badgers
And they're the Wolverines
Beth's last name is Patterson
Her age is 22
We both lived in Allenton
Before we came to you
Have you seen us?
Probably not
But just before we're tossed
If you have any info
Call 800-THE-LOST.

CULTURE

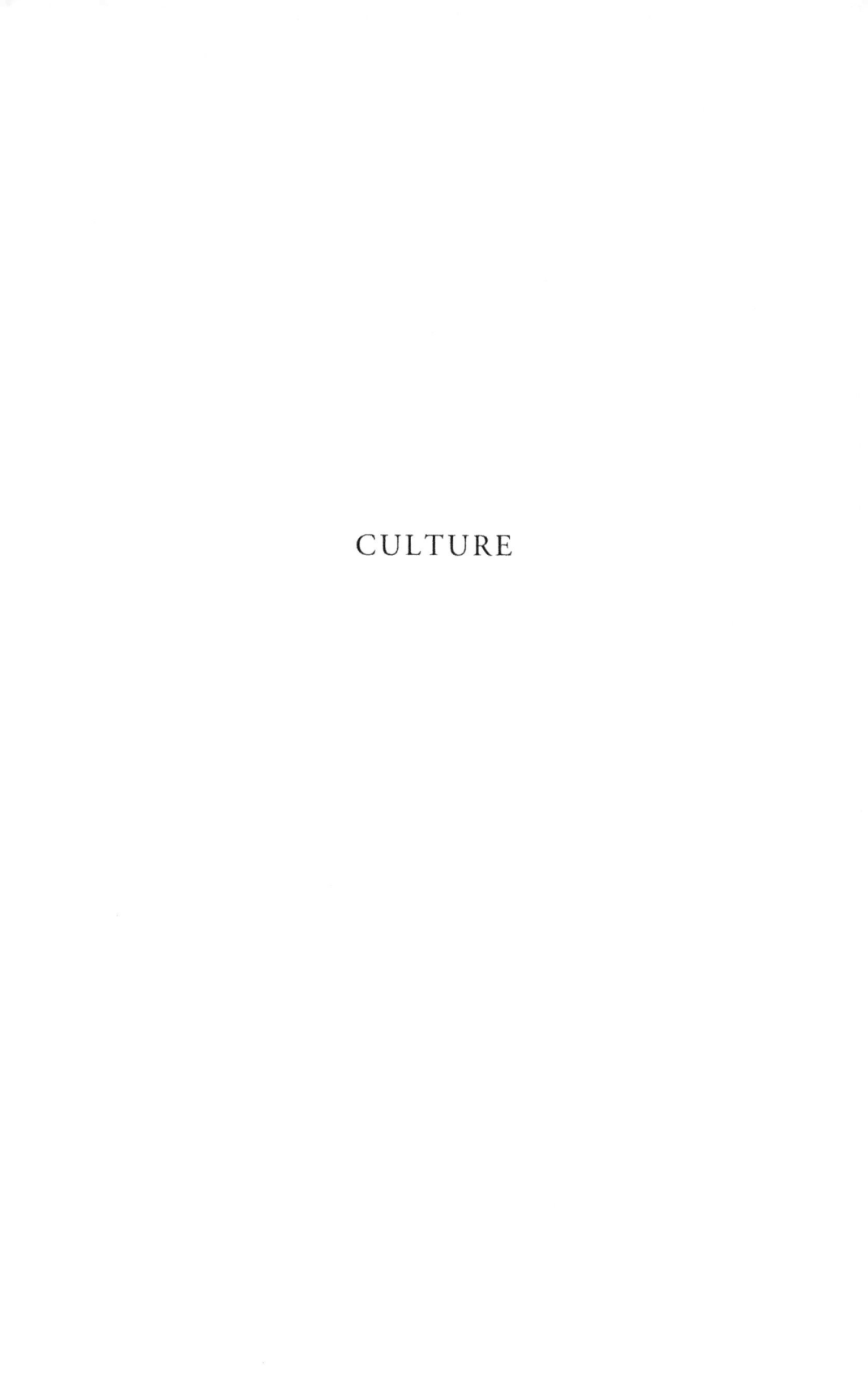

It's bad enough that human wedding ceremonies have reached obscene proportions. Now our pets are getting in on it. Destination wedding, Central Park?

Doghouse Deductions

Until I read yesterday about pet weddings, I was all set to build this week's column around income tax returns. Now I think I'll leave the Section 179 depreciation to my IRS auditor.

Yes, pet weddings. Source: the Sunday *Philadelphia Inquirer*. And if you need more proof that that paper's gone to the dogs, well, there it is.

Ah, yes. "Bow-wow vows." I suppose people with disposable income are entitled to spend it as they see fit. Some choose philanthropy; others, beach weddings in Oahu for their shih-tzu, Stumpy.

According to the article, there's a pet marriage counselor in Walla Walla WA who wants us to appreciate the significance of the ceremony for our canine couples: "Marriage for an animal is almost like marriage for a human."

Oh. Destined for divorce?

Actually, no, according to the counselor. "Nor do they require pre-niptuals." (Oof!)

This is not good news for the dog divorce attorneys out there. Someone should've advised them back in paw school that they'd do better as "car chasers."

Anyhow, it seems pet owners go to this Walla Walla woman for advice on whether or not the matches they've found for their pets should lead to – this is not my pun – muttrimony.

"This isn't an arranged marriage," she explains (despite what you just read in the previous paragraph about "the matches they've found for their pets"). "We can't force them together."

No. And they pick out their gown and tuxedo themselves, too.

The pet owners have the option of using a wedding planner for the ceremony or planning it themselves. If you happen to be invited to one of these events someday, don't worry about finding that perfect gift for the bride and groom.

PetSmart has a bridal registry.

One wedding organizer puts it this way: "We want to let people know that animals are human, too."

I'll give you a moment to let that one sink in before suggesting that, although humans are animals, it's been pretty much established that the converse isn't true – despite the reputed popularity of the Alley Cat at canine receptions.

And speaking of cats …

The principals in this piece about pet weddings were dogs. That is, if you ignore the humans who were quoted, and I think you'll agree with me that we should. But who says pet marriages should be limited to same-species animals? Don't lizards and crickets have rights, too?

My cat Deuce, a neutered male, is very fond of (that is, he tolerates) my ex-wife's German Shepherd, Xena, an alluring, spayed female about twenty times his size. Xena, in return, is gaga over Deuce. Now granted, consummating this relationship could be a problem, but shouldn't Xena and Deuce be as free to express their love as their same-species counterparts?

I think so.

Some pet owners, it seems, actually mate their pets because they don't want "illegitimate relations" in their home. (These are people who are still hoping Pat Robertson will run for president again.)

But take the case of Mac, our dearly departed male zebra finch. Mac spent his years in caged solitude, when here he could have tied the knot with Jincks, our equally departed male Brittany spaniel, and avoided the rumors swirling about their "love that speaks not its name."

But could he? I haven't read anything yet about same-sex inter-species wedlock, though somewhere in America, as we speak, somebody sees a market for it.

In closing, a word of advice for all our newlywed pooches: Get a good pet tax preparer and remember that it's generally more beneficial to file jointly.

In my boyhood, the only summer camp I attended was a day camp with activities such as swimming, arts and crafts, and getting picked on.

Summer Camps for Structured Lives

Last week, I was copyediting the *Summer Programs* brochure for my township. What jumped from the page at me, aside from some funny language ambiguities, was not only the proliferation of summer day camp offerings but also their unconventional nature. *Pony Grooming, Riding, and Horsemanship; Ultimate Roller Coaster; Super HERO Advocacy Program*. And, taking a cue from the popular "Survivor" television series, *SOS: Science of Survival*. ("Learn to make toothpaste from seaweed, construct a solar oven, build a shelter with handmade adobe bricks.")

Skills our middle schoolers might need when they're re-enacting *Lord of the Flies: Cape May* this summer.

There were lots more, and that wasn't even counting the sports programs, like *Cricket Clinic* and *The Mega Multi-Sports Camp*. The latter lets campers experience 15 different sports from around the world. (Register now! "Tsunami Dunk" and "Mexican Border Ball" fill up fast.)

Meanwhile, as I was busy marking up my copy and sowing linguistic elegance where there was once only grammatical chaos, 16 kids (15 girls and a boy – poor dude) were sitting in a makeshift classroom across the lobby from me. They were taking an all-day course to become certified babysitters.

An all-day course! To learn what? How to insert a DVD and make microwave popcorn? Oh, that's right, they might also have to master connecting the Xbox.

And their parents paid $60 for this?

Neither the oddball programs nor the certification class is a new phenomenon. The need for dual income parents to find summer programs to keep their kids occupied while they go to work has spawned day and overnight camps for seemingly every conceivable activity. And though I'm not sure what's with the certified-babysitter boom, it's a reality, and the classes are filled to capacity.

(I always thought the best "certification" was that the sitter lived close by.)

I know what's bothering me about all this: It's the *structure* goblin at it again. As if our kids' lives aren't structured enough.

In all my years as a parent, I've never asked my children to sign up for still more mental work in the summer after they've just done nine months of it in school. Math and science camps? More numbers? Here's a number for you – eight. As in Eighth Amendment. Cruel and unusual punishment.

Don't get me wrong; I'm no innocent. You want to see structure? Their mom and I schlepped them from one organized activity to the next as deftly and seamlessly as anyone we knew. Gymnastics, swimming lessons, all the ball sports, Mega Multi-Performing and Fine Arts Lessons ... Then there was that week-long seminar, *Be a Toddlerpreneur*, that we enrolled them in when they turned 2. And *Personal Investing: Even Ninja Turtles Need a 401(k)*. I remember that one, too. I still have that picture of them posing with Warren Buffett.

But we had the rare luxury of having a parent at home back then, which meant our kids could actually just hang out in summertime and play whatever and whenever they liked.

It's no coincidence that their fondest play memories have nothing to do with *Little League Sabermetrics* or *Be GRE GREat at 8*.

No, it's *Manhunt*. In the dark. Hands down. Certifiably.

INTERNATIONAL

"There's something new under the Sun!"

Wal-Martihuacan and Other Signs of the Apocalypse

Teotihuacan. "The place where the gods were created." Built in the first century BC by the Toltecs. Burned and destroyed in the seventh century. Reused by the Aztecs in the 13th century. Amortized by Sam Walton in the 21st century.

Huh?

Yes, Wal-Mart is opening a new store near the site of Mexico's 2000-year-old Pyramids of the Sun and Moon, and this is upsetting some people ("refrying their beans," as the Mayans used to put it).

But why?

When the pyramids were built, did anyone object to encroachment by developers? No. The 200-foot-tall Pyramid of the Sun was a stimulus to the local economy. It provided new, albeit short-lived, jobs for sacrificial virgins while creating a slew of ancillary occupations such as altar scrubbers, sacrifice disposal crews, and most importantly, high priests.

A key to the pyramid's success was its ability to buy the virgins in volume, and that economy of scale allowed an aggressive pricing policy that made it harder for the mom-and-pop pyramids to compete, forcing many of them to close their steps.

Inspired by the success of the Pyramid of the Sun, the Pyramid of the Moon opened as a members-only wholesale outlet called "Quetzalcoatl's Club," which enjoyed similar success.

With the decline of Teotihuacan, the pyramids were abandoned, leading to the phenomenon of big-box blight that plagues our own communities even today. Nature, however, had its own solution to the unsightliness caused by the abandoned buildings: It grew a jungle over them.

The new, 30-foot-tall Wal-Mart, (or, as it's called by the Teotihuacanadians, "casa lineas interminables") holds the promise of restoring Teotihuacan to its former glory and providing the same economic stimulus to the region as the Pyramids of the Sun and Moon once did centuries ago. Its earth tone exterior will combine with its bold, rectangular lines to produce a structure barely ... er, squarely ... in harmony with the ancient edifices.

The theme for Wal-Mart's Mexican ad campaign is "There's something new under the Sun!" The company chose that one because, as a senior advertising executive put it, "It's original."

A second indicator that the Apocalypse may be approaching is a nascent phenomenon that might best be described as "going into the closet."

A recent newspaper article talked about the 2,000 closet organizing companies in the country and the $2 billion that Americans spent remodeling their closets last year. One homebuilding company has a floor plan that comes with "a closet that's the length of a three-car garage, plus an additional walk-in closet." Customers are spending thousands of dollars to put such things in their closets as furniture-grade cherry cabinets, crown molding, and center islands.

And why?

Because their closets are a mess.

My favorite essayist, E.B. White, had this to say about our accumulation of clutter, or, as he called it, the "tides of acquisition:" "A home is like a reservoir equipped with a check valve: the valve permits influx but prevents outflow. ... Under ordinary circumstances, the only stuff that leaves a home is paper trash and garbage; everything else stays on and digs in."

Rather than purge the mess, people are remodeling their closets to hold the mess in a more organized fashion.

Making them look like dens, however, is another story. I say get rid of the mess and spend the closet money on a Mexican vacation to Teotihuacan, where, by the looks of things, the "tides of acquisition" are about to make land.

Vaccinations Not Necessary.

My Lawless Province Getaway

I was somewhat of a world traveler back in the day. From the familiar – Dublin, Paris, Copenhagen, Istanbul – to the unfamiliar – Erzurum, Mashad, Herat, Benares. I've trekked in the Himalayas, snorkeled in the Greek isles, and cruised the fjords in Norway.

There aren't many places on Earth I have an unfulfilled yearning to visit.

No, when it comes to travel, you're looking at a jaded man.

If I'm going to hit the open road again, my destination will have to be someplace a little more Exotic. Untamed. Raw. No Cancuns or Montego Bays for this guy. Honolulu may be for you-you but not for me-me.

That's why I've put my deposit down on two Club Ahmed weeks in Waziristan, one of Pakistan's "lawless provinces."

The brochure promises that I'll encounter "al-Qaeda forces and pro-Taliban groups."

Now we're talkin' travel.

The main tourist attraction there, naturally, is Osama bin Laden. I'd be disappointed if I didn't see him, having flown halfway around the world. But when you're traveling in the off-peak season, as I'll be, that's the risk you take.

The Club Ahmed travel rep tells me, though, that there's a decent chance of spotting Ayman al-Zawahiri, who is Osama's roommate and a bit more the social butterfly than his lanky companion. He and Osama can sometimes be seen together knocking a few down at the Khyber Pass Lounge on the main drag in Razmak, where, according to the locals, they're an unbeatable shuffleboard team.

Look, I'm a realist. I'm not getting my hopes up about running into either of them. There's an autographed photo of the two of them signing the guest book at the front desk of the hotel where I'll be staying in Darpa Khel. That may be the closest I'll come to actually seeing them.

You never want to build your trip to a foreign country around one tourist attraction anyway, because things happen. You might be sick that day, or the weather might be bad. If I see bin Laden, fine. If not, there's lots else to do in Waziristan.

One of the main tourist attractions for male travelers like me is the chance to head my very own Waziri household. It's an extremely conservative area, Waziristan. Women are carefully guarded, and every household must be headed by a male figure. There's this "Who Wears the Pants?" package, with options ranging from 24 hours all the way up to heading a household for the entire month of Ramadan. The few guys who have done it say that the one-month experience is "unforgettable."

Buzkashi, the national sport of Afghanistan, is also immensely popular in Waziristan. That's the game in which two teams on horseback compete to gain possession of a headless goat carcass. They can spend days riding back and forth across a large plain, battling over the carcass like a swarm of six-year-old soccer players until one team succeeds in dropping what's left of it into the scoring area. All the while, lawless spectators are wagering and shouting Waziri cheers such as "Push 'em back, shove 'em back, way back to Rawalpindi!" and "Hold that ram!"

The annual al-Qaeda vs. Taliban Buzkashi match is considered a must-see sporting event, and I've been fortunate enough to get a ticket at midfield on longitude line 71ºE, which happens to be the border between Pakistan and Afghanistan. The game's fiercely competitive nature results in both the al-Qaeda and the Taliban squads crossing back and forth between countries frequently in the course of the match, so I'll see a lot of the action.

Afterward, I'm going to try for a picture of me posing with some of the al-Qaeda players. (The Taliban are opposed to cameras and won't allow them inside their locker room.)

Then, time permitting, I'll take a day trip over to Kabul, riding with the locals on one of those colorfully festooned Afghani buses. I'll add to the color by wearing my Yankees baseball cap, the one that announces to everyone, "Look at me. I'm an American!"

A dynamite ending to a getaway adventure.

FALALA

All that was missing was the line "Wanna come back to my crib?"

As Crèches Go

As crèches go, this one was pretty impressive, so much so that I had to stop and look. I was driving past it in downtown Philadelphia when something moving caught my eye.

It's not every day, or every Christmas, that you see live animals in the Nativity scene, but there they were: a donkey, a cow, and four sheep, grazing and lazing in a foot-thick bed of hay.

Passersby had stopped with their wide-eyed children to become part of the crèche action, and the tots were eagerly rubbing the livestock.

I called it Jesus's Petting Zoo.

Problem was, a key story element was missing.

Where in the world was Baby Jesus? (*Dove è il Bambino Gesù?* I could hear Pavarotti singing.)

The manger, normally a feeding trough when not a baby repository, was conspicuously empty.

Nevertheless, Mary was in her standard crèche location, gazing down on it. She was surrounded there in the stable by six guys looking shepherdish (antonym of "sheepish"). Except for the one in the corner in gold lamé. He didn't fit any shepherd description I knew of. By the gilded looks of him, he had to be one of the Magi, but where were his pals?

Maybe they had to change camels in Lebanon.

One of the other five must have been Joseph, but your guess was as good as mine as to which one. This is where those peel-off name tags would've come in handy.

All the figures were life-size, and for a moment I thought I was looking at a troupe of performance artists, like the costumed ones you see in frozen poses on the streets of Paris. But they were just mannequins.

Still, it looked more like a scene at a pickup bar ("The Stable") than the most sacred childbirth tableau in Western civilization.

With a six-to-one guy-to-chick ratio.

With two days to go before Christmas, I could understand the manger being vacant. Mary hadn't even gone into labor by that time. Verisimilitude, I believe, is the term for it: the appearance of being true or real. The look on her face said, "When is my water going to break for God's sake?" even though it was humanity's sake it was going to break for.

But what was a Wise Man doing in the picture? And even though he wasn't, really, wasn't it time to give Joseph his props as the true father among these agro-gigolos in their coats of many colors hitting on the beatific Mary? ("Hail, Mary.")

It was as though two separate companies had been awarded the crèche contract, and the one that got the outside job came in under deadline but the one handling the inside work was unionized. ("Look, Joseph is not my responsibility. I just do the shepherds.")

It would be interesting to return to the crèche in a few days to see if the stable occupants have sorted out their personal space issues and established a pecking order, and, of course, to see the star attraction Himself, but one thing's for sure -- if the profound disinterest they exhibited today is any indication, the animals in attendance will be far more preoccupied with the hay outside than with the "Hey!" inside causing all the fuss.

This is a piece about thrift at the micro and macro levels, inspired by the language of Christmas.

"Tinsel"? or "Icicles"?

Families use language in keeping with their unique traditions. At Thanksgiving, my mother made the "filling," while, in Bethlehem, PA, my wife's mother was making the "stuffing." Today, we "decorated" our Christmas tree. Elsewhere, some other family "trimmed" theirs.

"Trimming a tree" has multiple connotations. I doubt that was my parents' reason for not using the term, but it's certainly mine. Why use an ambiguous word when there are so many exact ones out there?

All of which is but a lead-up to a Christmas recollection I had today while decorating our tree. Over the years, as we've accumulated a store of ornaments having sentimental and aesthetic value, we as a family have gotten away from using that old standby, tinsel, in our tree-decorating scheme. Between static electricity, children, and the dog, most of it comes off the tree anyway, and we've all experienced how it seems to reproduce once it hits the floor. Like fruit flies, just when you think you got the last one, another one shows up.

But today I thought of tinsel. Immutable, problematic tinsel. The tinsel of my childhood (In our family, we called it "icicles.")

And I remembered that, each year, we saved the used tinsel to put on the following year's tree.

No, not every strand. We were cheap, not anal.

Or were we cheap? Poor was probably more like it.

In WalMart you can get tinsel for fifty cents a box. But my mother saved ours to use again.

I once heard a counselor say, "We're loyal to systems." And I was, adhering to my mother's practice for more years than I care to admit. It's like the story of the mother whose daughter asks her why she always cut the ends off the ham before putting it in the baking pan. The mother says, "I don't know. That's what *my* mother did." And *she* asks *her* mother, who gives the same response. And so on back to the great-grandmother who started the tradition, and her response is, "Because the pan was too small."

When I think of my tinsel-recycling childhood, I recall other symbols of a modest, blue-collar upbringing. Foremost was our near-total reliance on public transportation. Neither of my parents learned to drive or owned a car, so buses, trolleys, the subway, and the el were how we got around. I'm long removed from those days now, but in Philadelphia alone, tens of thousands of people rely on public transportation daily to get them to and from the workplace, or school, or shopping.

Their hard lives just got harder this week when SEPTA, the region's transit authority, announced that it was raising fares *and* cutting service. Fifty cents might buy you a box of tinsel, but it also equals a 25% fare hike for people who, if they could afford to, would much prefer living out here with us car owners.

Taking public transportation is no bowl of figgy pudding. Standing on street corners waiting for the bus. Jostling to get onto the bus. Standing after you do get on. Escalators that don't work. Grouchy cashiers. The constant sense of needing to be on your guard.

People don't use public transportation because they want to. They use it because they have to. And now they'll pay more and wait longer for the privilege.

The Philadelphia mayor demonstrated sympathy for the plight of his mass-transit constituents when he begged the SEPTA board to at least put off the inevitable announcement until after Christmas.

His request was not honored.

I don't want to get into the economic and political reasons why public transportation is in such bad shape. I'm just following a train of thought here that began with a reminiscence about being chintzy over tinsel. But it's good for us to remember now and then that, for every Currier & Ives or Hallmark idealization of Christmas, there are a hundred hardscrabble ones in the Dickens mold, whose Mr. Scrooge would find kindred spirits on the SEPTA board and, yes, in my goodly, tinsel-saving mother.

PITS

A dog story. A sad story.

Rupert's Gift

The scratch begins just beneath the rear passenger window. It arcs the length of Rupert's stiletto tail before the sweep of the door panel dictates the beginning of the end of its path.

Rupert, my son's dog, put it there. An inadvertent brushstroke on a sheet metal canvas.

Body work of a sort.

Exuberant even in his frailty, he left it there for me in his zeal for the back seat. Too big not to notice yet too superficial to do anything about, it's my indelible Rupert autograph. That, along with a few rug stains, the by-product of his illness.

He is sick, mysteriously so. A month ago, my son Nick, a Pitt fifth-year senior, asked if I could take him for a few weeks in July so Nick could concentrate on finishing his final three classes to graduate. I said sure, who wouldn't want to have Rupert for company? But in the interim, he began failing to keep his food down and was urinating frequently. Two veterinary clinics in Pittsburgh were unable to diagnose the problem despite x-rays, stool and urine samples, and a battery of blood work.

By the time Nick arrived here last weekend with Rupert, the dog had lost a fourth of his body weight and was utterly anorexic. His collar was hanging from his once-thick neck like a juggler's hoop. At our local veterinary hospital, additional blood tests were negative, but an abdominal ultrasound suggested something going on in his intestinal tract.

This morning, he's undergoing exploratory surgery, while Nick is back in Pittsburgh, powerless and scared for his dog's well-being.

Like Gelsomina, the strongman's assistant in Fellini's *La Strada*, Rupert's visage possesses a forlorn quality, a gentle inscrutableness that compels affection. He doesn't have to perform or do anything to engender this response. Using a blood type analogy, he's a "universal recipient": There's no one who meets him who doesn't give him love.

From the day he brought this five-month-old puppy home from the rescue shelter, Nick allowed Rupert to sleep with him in his bed and snuggle with him on the couch. So when he's with me, that's what we do, too. If you're on the couch and he knows you, you've got yourself a 45-pounds-of-pure-muscle lapdog.

During the past week, I've spent a lot of time with Rupert. Just him and me. My whole world right now, at least all that matters of it, is here in my house with him.

I've learned how to give him daily penicillin injections, but they don't seem to be making a difference. He's been refusing food the past two days, except last night, when he wanly stared me into giving him some of my Whopper.

Show him his leash, however, and he transforms into The Old Rupert. Take him for a walk and only his bony appearance would tell you something isn't right.

Rupe sleeps in his crate, next to my bed. He's been too weak to scale my mattress, or even the couch, so you *know* he's sick. No one wants to inflict surgery on a beloved pet, but you're glad it's an option when there are no other answers.

Nick's mom and I talked the other day about the mounting costs for all these tests and procedures. In discussions like that, someone's going to play the devil's advocate and say, "After all, it's just a dog. It'd be different if it was your child." But lying on the floor next to him, trying with single-minded tenderness to soothe him through his pain, I know that "just a dog" belies the real truth.

It's not a question of a dog's life being less valuable than a human life. If it were, I'd care more about my brother-in-law's step-daughter's toddler than I do about Rupert. But the former barely moves the needle, so peripheral is he to my daily life.

No, the reality is that, animal or human, intensity of feeling is proportionate to the level of connectedness. Rupe has been constancy and companionship for my son for three years and a frequent guest at my house, leaving only happiness – and a few coverless baseballs – as his calling card.

He is as central to our lives as our family dog Jincks used to be – back when we were a family.

10:00 a.m.: The vet calls to tell me she's found a foreign object in Rupert's small intestine. She'll remove it, flush out the abdomen, and close him up. I'm ecstatic and immediately call Nick with the news. He's elated, the relief in his voice palpable.

I email his mother the news. "EXCELLENT!! What a relief!" she writes back. But not before I get a second call.

10:18 a.m: It's the vet again – to report Rupert's in recovery, I'm thinking. "While we were closing him up," she tells me, "his heart stopped. We're trying to revive him right now. I'll call you back."

Rocked and barely able to speak, I'm stammering "Please get him back." I can't say the word "die."

Sometimes we're given the chance to pray for intervention; other times it's too late. Until I hear back from her, I will not stop beseeching God for Rupert's life. The passionless inadequacy of "Not my will, but thine" – what I've been schooled to pray for – is never more apparent to me.

I'm calling out to Rupert, picturing him as he was before the illness, when there was such strength in his potent body. Jaws clenched around his leash, his powerful neck muscles trying to whipsaw it into submission. A hilarious sight.

I'm calling out to him, exhorting, sending this essence-of-Rupert picture of him with all my heart to *his* heart, so he'll know somehow and remember the strength he possessed and clamp those jaws down on Death and fling him away.

No. I will not stop until I hear from her – one way or the other.

The phone rings. I pick up. "We tried, five of us tried ... We couldn't bring him back ... I'm sorry."

That morning, before he put the scratch on my car as we were leaving for the vet, I walked him to the end of the block and back. His tail was wagging, his head held high.

He rode the four miles to the vet with his head out the back window, at one with the racing air. Before bringing him in, I walked with him a last time through a nearby field made lovely by a swath of wild grasses. They intrigued him.

When it was time to go, we walked together from the field to the building's entrance. As ever, his leash was in his mouth.

Inside, he let a trio of small children play with him until the staff person came to take him.

I handed him over with a final, encouraging rub of his fur, never expecting that he wouldn't be coming back.

Rupert was three and a half, and there aren't enough tears in the world for this one.

Especially in Pittsburgh.

When I ask people about their dogs, it's heartening how frequently the reply is "(S)he's a rescue dog."

A New York Doll

This story's about Noell.

Noell is one of two dogs, along with Jazz, that belong to my sons Nick and John, respectively. They are pit bulls, a breed about which little positive is said or written.

For that reason alone, I'm proud of my boys for seeing past the (too often justified) negative image and taking a chance on discovering how incredibly affectionate these dogs can be. They love to be in contact with humans ("Yeah, with their teeth," some of you are thinking; well, don't be cynical and hear me out.) They will lick your face endlessly and will sleep with you if you let them.

Sounds like me.

Both Noell and Jazz are rescue dogs. Noell was 4 when Nick adopted her two years ago, after his first rescued pit bull, Rupert, adopted when Nick was a student at Pitt, did not survive surgery for an obstructed intestine.

Noell's story, as told to Nick, is that she had suffered not so much from abuse as from indifference. The distinction is perhaps only a matter of degree, or semantics. Never allowed indoors by the owner, she has on her underbelly a permanent patch of rough, darkened, frostbitten-looking skin from sleeping on pavement. She was found unclaimed, lying in the street in New York City, her leg broken after being hit by a car.

Noell is engaging and she welcomes affection, yet her earlier circumstances have clearly affected her demeanor. She appears to slip at times into what looks almost like melancholy, her doleful eyes and bearing reflecting the residual effects of an animal that's been ground down.

I learned something else about her this week.

She's staying with me while Nick's on vacation – I watch the dogs so I'll get paid back in grandchildren – and I'm head-over-heels in love with this gentle creature. Yesterday, after walking her, I thought she might enjoy that most basic of canine aerobic activities: Fetch. I picked up a piece of branch about a foot and a half long and flung it across my yard.

Noell didn't budge.

Okay, maybe she's not used to this game, I thought. So I did what any human participant in Fetch would do: I carried the stick over to her so she could examine it, expecting she'd piece together what she was supposed to do and off she'd go, fetching, or some approximation of it.

But this was not what Noell did. Instead, as I approached her with the stick, her left eye, the one closest to me, closed protectively and her whole body flinched and tensed, shrinking from some anticipated pain.

I knew immediately that "indifference" wasn't all this beautiful animal had been subjected to.

Seeing her cower like that changed everything between us. Before, I was merely entertaining her, getting to know her, but now, in what felt like a form of conversion, I was driven to give her all the love and physical contact that I could in the time she was with me. Pure compassion enveloped me, which is one of the blessings of growing older.

It's something we can't explain. Some call it God's will: two lonely, rejected pit bulls, one in Pittsburgh, the other in New York City, and a young man who had the heart and the courage to assume responsibility for their care. Their destinies were intertwined. The heartbreak of Rupert's untimely death released the latch on a shelter door, where poor Noell was caged … and transformed her life.

While her affection for humans was unrelenting, Jazz would have preferred to be the only dog on this planet.

My "Jazz"-ercise Workout

My youngest son's dog Jazz is a 2-year-old rescued pit bull full of love and affection and bits of ears from other dogs. Today we are out walking together.

One surefire way to get a head count of the dogs in your neighborhood that are allowed to be off-leash is to walk a dog capable of separating them from their ears. Invariably, the free-rangers will head straight for the animal at the end of your leash, the Mike-Tyson-with-tags you *so* don't want them near.

For example, here comes "Kelly," who looks to have a little pit bull in her herself. Kelly has bounded off her front porch to learn more about Jazz.

I wish she'd direct her inquiries to me.

I would tell Kelly how Jazz recently had an incident with my oldest son's dog Noell. A female-on-female thing. Noell had to have surgery next morning to save her ear, and Jazz had to be quarantined for ten days, which basically means, as the county health department worker cheerily told me, "Oh, sure, you can walk her, but keep her on a tight leash."

Their altercation was over a guy – me. Both dogs were staying at my house – long story – and they were so happy to see me when I came in one night that they were competing for my attention like two teenage girls at the lifeguard stand. That changed in a flash when Jazz went all feral on Noell.

With that as background, let's return to Kelly, who is showing no signs of listening to her owner's cries of "Here, Kelly. C'mon, Kelly." The Cautious Me thinks better of letting them meet. I lift Jazz by her harness, a truly magnificent invention, and position myself between her and the rapidly closing Kelly, just as I had with Jazz and Noell on the Night of the Long Fangs. Will I never learn?

Kelly, meanwhile, reminds me of the Irishman returning home to his ill-natured wife after a night at the pub, unlocking the door and not knowing "what he was letting himself in for." Every advance of her eager, friendly paws ratchets up my stress level. I'm calling out urgently in the direction of the owner's voice, whom I can't even see, "Please control your dog!" Just when it appears that nothing is going to get Kelly to turn back, her owner's command registers and she returns to her porch. The street beneath my feet is drenched in sweat.

"She won't hurt you. She's harmless," Kelly's owner's voice assures me.

"It's not your dog I'm worried about," I respond, as it suddenly dawns on this person how close Kelly may have just come to reconstructive surgery.

"Thank you," is her heartfelt answer to me, the beneficent, nerve-rattled dog walker.

Not twenty yards further into our walk, another leash-less canine crosses the street in front of us. This one looks old. I do not want to learn if Jazz does better with old dogs, so we do a quick 180 past Kelly again before Jazz even realizes a senior citizen was in her path.

At the end of the next block there's an energetic border collie – Is there any other kind? – playing with her owner along the side of their house. I would like to be thinking, "How cute," but instead it's "Get a @!%#-ing leash on her, will ya!" as my diastolic bumps up another ten points. I steal past with Jazz, like a scouting party behind enemy lines, praying that we escape her attention. The last thing we need is to be herded.

Until you're a dog owner, even an acting one like me, you don't realize how many of them live in your neighborhood, leashed or not leashed. Not to worry, though. A dog must be walked, and that creates a scent, which draws the attention of every mutt and purebred along the route. The barking frenzy that follows makes dog counting an easy task.

For instance, I now know that there are 27 dogs along my one-mile route. With all due respect to cat lovers, your feline pets simply do not provide this sort of good demographic information.

But as for the idiots who think that, just because their dogs are benign, there's no need to keep them on a leash, I suggest they rethink that approach … unless they're looking for a reason to rename their pet "Van Gogh."

FINDINGS III

Where but in Harper's Findings can you learn that the magic number may be four?

Unicorns in North Korea? Why Not?

Back when I wrote a weekly column for the *New Hope Gazette*, a regular feature in *Harper's* magazine called "Findings" was reliable fodder for my creative juices. The "findings" on the Findings page are primarily investigative and come largely from the natural and the social sciences. These discoveries, inventions and observations about our world are presented in a matter-of-fact style using simple declarative sentences.

As it happens, many of them are hilarious.

I pick out the ones I like best and comment on them. This current list is from the February 2013 issue. Dive in and match the finding with its corresponding comment. Answers appear at the bottom. Best, I think, to read the Findings in their entirety first, then take the Comments one at a time.

FINDINGS

    A. A student sued her university for failing to accommodate her allergies to cactuses, escalators, tall people, and mauve.
    B. No new poisons were found in Tycho Brahe's beard.
    C. In Grapeland, Texas, a ring-tailed lemur named Keanu attacked a postwoman named Reeves.
    D. North Korean archaeologists confirmed the discovery of a unicorn lair.
    E. Lying increases the temperature of the nose.
    F. A wandering mind shortens one's telomeres.
    G. Neurobiologists created white smell.
    H. Biochemists blocked the gene that allows fruit flies to perceive the gentle stroking of a human eyelash.
    I. Hip injuries are widespread among swans.
    J. The magic number may be four.

K. Carp at Czech Christmas markets align themselves along a north-south axis.
L. Traditional sales-pitching was dying out in Britain.
M. Dogs were found to exhibit no inherent shape biases.
N. Canadians were found likelier to spend money that looks dirty.

COMMENTS

1. It's why Geppetto had to install central air in his workshop.
2. During Holy Week, however, they go west-to-Easter.
3. But they did over time betray a tendency to be skeptical of trapezoids.
4. Anything to avoid paying off her student loans.
5. Prompting a sharp decline in white noise futures.
6. Had she died in the attack, it would've been a case of matricide.
7. But it's been immortalized in the London stage production of Artie Miller's "Death of a Traditional Salesman."
8. They were led there on a tip from Kim Jong-Un's guest, Dennis Rodman.
9. Turns out the evidence that he was poisoned was only antidotal.
10. When it's not busy broadening one's horizons.
11. "Ah," said the fruit fly, "that feels to me like the gentle stroking of a hu ..." ZAP!
12. The Swiss, on the other hand, were found likelier to launder it.
13. Except during Daylight Saving Time, when it's five.
14. Well, no wonder you never see them walking.

ANSWERS: 1-E, 2-K, 3-M, 4-A, 5-G, 6-C, 7-L, 8-D, 9-B, 10-F, 11-H, 12-N, 13-J, 14-I

EVERYDAY THINGS

When first this column was launched, the editor christened it with a title I found as anemic as a dialysis patient. But who was I, a newbie, to question his wisdom? Three years later, I spoke up.

They Can't Place the Face

I once got an email from a reader who said, "You sound cute. Are you?" Another reader wrote, "If there were a photo of you on the page, I wouldn't have to read so many words."

I feel their frustration. All each of them wanted was a picture of me. Is that asking too much, to see the face behind the drivel?

Most columns these days are accompanied by a headshot, or a thumbnail of a headshot, or, in your grooming-oriented publications, a headshot of a thumbnail. In any case, I'm not sure what the holdup is. The *Gazette* snapped a photo of me over two years ago, when the paper's parent company was preparing to include headshots for all its columnists.

After that, nothing happened (ironic pause).

So there's the headshot issue bugging me, its resolution long overdue. But while I'm at it, this "Everyday Things" column name they stuck me with has to go, too. I'd have said something about it sooner, but with the Delaware flooding three times in two years, my divorce, and sordid, sorry . . . *assorted* . . . other developments going on, I didn't see it as a hot-button issue.

So what if readers have reported falling asleep on the spot when they see it, like a narcoleptic version of Monty Python's "World's Funniest Joke?"

So what if an unbiased Ingrid and Oodvar Norsjk, of Lumberville, petitioned to change their town's name to "Slumberville" after only two exposures to "Everyday Things?"

You know what they say about everyday things, don't you? "It's the everyday things that'll kill you." Or, as the Norsjks themselves would put it, "It's the everyday things that'll kill yoü."

"Everyday Things" has no positive connotations. When I hear the words, I think humdrum, repetitive, mundane. Thoreau's "lives of quiet desperation" mixed with dry dog food.

I didn't ask for the title; it was given to me. And looking back at various topics I've covered, sure, I've dabbled in the ordinary. Who could be more ordinary than Information Technology Man or Megawati Sukarnoputri? And what about Blackie the Missing Pet Crow?

But in my defense, I think I'm decidedly more drawn to the unconventional and the offbeat. Take the pieces I wrote on Thanksgiving, pets, and baseball. And I've been Nancy Grace-like in pursuit of the naked half-truths behind titillating topics like plastic wrap, multiplication tables, and high school reunions ... and maybe the most risqué of them all – clutter.

So I really think it's unfair that I've been shackled all this time with a title as bogus and disingenuous as "Everyday Things."

That's right, powers-that-be, you heard me: bogus and disingenuous.

Therefore, I am hereby mounting a double-edged campaign: I want the headshot I was promised *and* a new name for my column.

If we put our heads together (that'd be a headshot!), I'm sure we can produce a hundred names more inspiring than Ev ... I can't even bring myself to say it again.

I am so confident that this creative, artistic community can come up with something better that, at the risk of receiving responses on the order of "Who Cares?" or "Ulysses!", I am inviting you to send in your ideas to the email address listed below.

I promise I'll print the best of them, as selected by a neutral pair of Scandinavian judges from Lumberville.

And while you're at it, lobby the newspaper for headshots.

Then you'll see what "cute" really is.

ACKNOWLEDGEMENTS

First, unquestionably, I want to recognize and embrace my three kids – Nick, Chloe, and John – for their perceptive advice, editorial input, and technical assistance in helping me bring this collection to life. They "surround me with their boundless love," as the great John Prine expressed it.

A nod, too, to one of the family, Kellie Kovac, for her cover art and design. Is there a more endearing Thinker Sloth than the one she created? I'd have to think about that.

I also send a shout-out to former *Gazette* editors Scott Edwards and Daniel Brooks for their appreciation and support for my work. There is such talent, kindness, and care for the community in those two individuals. Scott, you opened a new, creative door for me when you welcomed me to the paper. And Dan, who knew that getting my own headshot would be so effortless once you arrived? And you both were great when I missed a deadline … which was NEVER. Boo-yah!

And to my readers:

New Hope is not a large place, but it has a large reach creatively and geographically as a magnet for the arts. I'm overjoyed to have been a part of the town's energy in my years of engaging with you from the pages of the *Gazette*. As the pieces in this collection have hopefully revealed, I strove to aim high and never write down to you. Besides, you wouldn't have stood for it. We were a good fit that way. I gave you my best shot week in and week out, and you gave me your receptivity in return.

ABOUT THE AUTHOR

For five years, until the newspaper's demise, John Shields wrote a weekly commentary page column for the *New Hope Gazette*, a publication that put him in the heart, and the tradition, of literary-rich Bucks County, Pennsylvania. This summer, he marked a miraculous milestone in his life with his 30th anniversary as a kidney transplant recipient. That transforming experience, along with those gained as a teacher, healthcare administrator, stay-at-home dad, varsity baseball head coach, and frequent guest at area operating rooms, provided a unique frame of reference for his work.

John has a bachelor's degree in English from St. Joseph's University, a teacher certification in secondary school English (also from St. Joseph's), and an MBA in Health Administration from Temple University. He is a father of three, one of whom, Chloe, is the mother of his glorious granddaughter, Nora.

John was a performing singer/songwriter/guitarist in his day, and, simply put, words and music are key elements in his life. Retired from column writing, he sees a memoir in his future. Meanwhile, he remains active musically, performing standards from the 1920s-1950s for residents of senior care facilities.

A native Philadelphian, John now lives in Hatboro, PA, one of the only places in America named after an apparel accessory – if you don't count the Beltway.

Made in the USA
Coppell, TX
10 January 2021